LIDO

LIDO

A dip into outdoor swimming pools:
the history, design and people behind them

Christopher Beanland

BATSFORD

First published in the United Kingdom in 2020
by Batsford
43 Great Ormond Street
London WC1N 3HZ

An imprint of B. T. Batsford Holdings Limited

ISBN: 9781849945844

A CIP catalogue record for this book is
available from the British Library.

10 9 8 7 6 5 4 3 2

Reproduction by Rival Colour Ltd, UK
Printed by Leo Paper Products Ltd, China

This book can be ordered direct from
the publisher at the website:
www.batsfordbooks.com or try
your local bookshop.

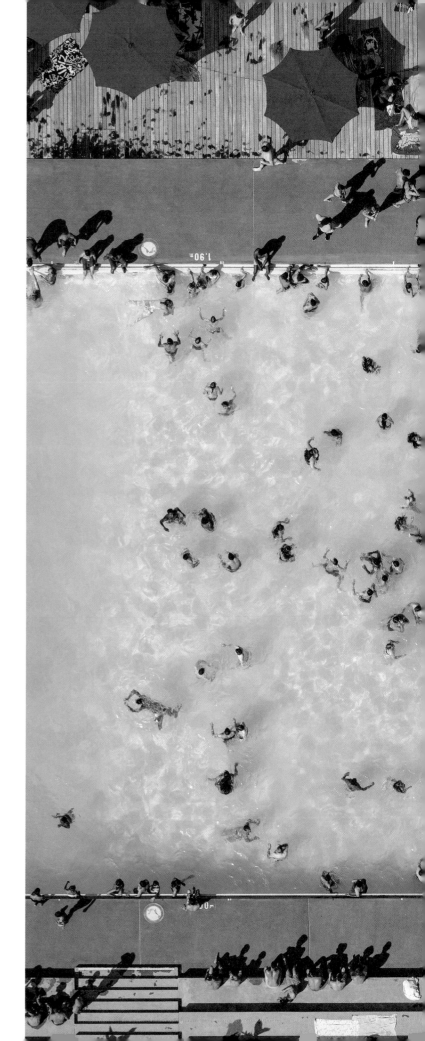

CONTENTS

Introduction

To swim is to be reborn. Each dive into the water is a leap of faith. Each stroke draws you closer to some nebulous goal. Each breath reinforces your sense of sentient humanity. Swimming produces a new swimmer – a fresher, healthier, stronger, mentally cleansed version of the person who arrived with a head full of thoughts but will leave with only one: 'It's time to eat cake'. Literature, film and the therapy-soaked everyday lives of the Western middle class are all awash with the idea of renewal. By jumping into the pool you can often obtain redemption for the same price as a coffee.

Swimming is recreation as ritual. The imagery is obvious enough: water comforts us because it's the nearest thing we have to being back inside the womb. The religious iconography of immersion and blessing is in play too. And maybe there's something dragging us back to the time when our forebears first wriggled out of the sea and on to the land. Perhaps the water never left our souls when it left our lungs. The first public pool was probably the Great Bath at Mohenjo-daro in today's Pakistan. This 5,000-year-old remnant of that great city of the Indus Valley

civilization looks, in many ways, just like today's pools. The Greeks and Romans also swam and bathed, as did the Egyptians and Japanese. Ottoman hammams offered relaxation and 18th-century mineral spas in the Anglo and Teutonic worlds (Bath, Baden-Baden, Karlovy Vary) promised to cure ills before beta blockers and erythromycin. But until the 1900s swimming for fun was rare. Baths were primarily places to wash – the name has lived on in England's northern industrial towns and England's southern hemisphere colonies, where going to the baths today means going for a swim, not to wash. But those bath days were also time for a little relaxation in strained existences.

That mass washing of the 1800s and 1900s is worth noting because it laid a foundation for pool time being about leisure as well as lengths, about frolicking in the water too. Homes, Western ones at least, are all now built with bathrooms. But the camaraderie of bath day lives on at modern lidos where time by the side of the pool is as much a part of the experience as time in the water. Munching snacks, reading novels, painting nails and scrolling through dating apps are big poolside favourites today.

Competitive swimming grew in popularity throughout the 1800s, culminating in its inclusion in the Olympics for the first time at Athens in 1896. Frantic laps and race training became normalized at the pool. Slowly, pools also became places in which to get fit. The 20th century was in some ways the apogee of the swimming pool. The Victorians fetishized death and ignored sex. Now it was to be the other way around. Sex and exercise make you feel more alive than anything else. Trailblazers like Jersey's 1895 Havre des Pas Pool kicked off this new era of pool building as the people's century swept away millennia of stagnation.

Modernism, among its many and varied clarion calls, made the case for health and efficiency. The swimming pool was of course an intrinsic part of this: to be clean, lean, outdoors; for ordinary people to access exercise and enjoyment; for all this to take place in buildings whose form followed function; and where detail was sparing and well chosen. Especially in the 1920s and '30s, public pools of an often impressive size sprung up hither and thither, like Lyons Pool in Staten Island, New York. Le Corbusier missed a trick – the pool squeezed into the middle of the rooftop running track on top of the Unité d'Habitation in Marseille is only deep enough for kids to paddle in, rather than people to dive into. Lubetkin made the pool at Highpoint in North London big enough for lengths, although it doesn't quite have the wow factor of the pool for the penguins he designed at nearby London Zoo.

Art deco became a recurring theme of many of these endeavours, especially along England's south coast in places like Saltdean, Penzance and Margate. The English seaside is that most perplexing of places – everybody goes there but no one swims in the sea.

Pools next to the sea are strange. Pools play the essential role of sea-substitute in grossly landlocked cities like Almaty in Kazakhstan, where half the population will die without ever having seen the coast. Australian pools often featured brick buildings but reinforced concrete played a part in other places. Its influence was keenly felt with diving board towers, kind of proto-motorway sliproads in the sky. The boards at the Tropicana in Weston-super-Mare (which hosted Banksy's satirical Dismaland exhibition in 2015) by H. A. Brown (demolished 1982), João Batista Vilanova Artigas' brutalist 1960 platform in Rio de Janeiro and the diving board at the Tivoli in Innsbruck by N. Heltschl, from 1964, expressed their structural truism.

The last of the great modernist pools came with Brisbane's Centenary Baths in 1959, with a Jetsons-style pavilion overlooking the water. Aussies never fell out of love with their pools. In Northern Europe and North America bathing beauties contests and packed pools gave way to bargain beach breaks that lured people to sunnier climes like Mallorca and Cancun in the *Mad Men* era, and strange social shifts took place. In the UK, the welfare state was at its high point in the 1970s with millions calling council houses homes and high-quality free healthcare for all. Yet, many lifestyles were far from healthy – with heavy drinking and smoking being the norm for some. All this, combined with a loss of faith in anything 'municipal' – and what were public pools if not that? – led to a slump and many closures throughout the 1980s. Their occasional replacements in the linen suit and cocaine age were the wave pools and leisure centres with slides – always at least partly under cover, as if swimming, like shopping, had moved from high street and market to supermarket and supermall – because we wanted to drive to both swim and shop, and stay dry when wet, apparently.

Things have changed dramatically today. Wellness is a new religion, 20 lengths before breakfast the natural corollary. Pools are cool according to the tiresome articles (oh wait, I wrote one) in newspapers' glossy magazines (though when were they not?). In countries like Germany the tradition never really went away. Their (as the English would see it) pathological attitude to nudity and an *Aufguss* addiction, combined with everything else being shut on a Sunday, has always ensured a plethora of pool/spas doing business in every Teutonic town and city.

Like so much in the sphere of architecture, pools can convey a great deal. As with housing, they can connote elitism or democracy. Here we are concerning ourselves mostly, but not entirely, with public pools. Public pools are peoples' spaces. That's why they are busy. As with hotels' eerie gyms, hotel pools are always empty, unless it's August and you're in a package holiday hotspot on the Mediterranean coast. Home pools' emptiness is more spooky still – no wonder François Ozon was inspired to make his 2003 *film dramatique, Swimming Pool*. The drained backyard pool is a recurring image in J. G. Ballard's writing. In the movie of *Empire of The Sun*, the empty pool is especially unforgettable.

But public pools stay busy. Rules are there to be followed. And like on trains, to wit there is a baroque performance where we learn how to interact and share space with strangers, sometimes in challenging, sweaty circumstances. The lifeguard's whistle going off is the universal sonic symbol of an infraction; lane discipline, shower discipline, towel placement discipline, no ducking, no bombing,

no horseplay, no petting. Australian writer Ellen Savage says this all 'stands in for some of the more frightening elements of our rule-by-consent-of-the-ruled society' in an article for *Kill Your Darlings*. She also wisely points to Michel Foucault's idea of heterotopia, the weird world in microcosm. The lido is a perfect example of a heterotopia, sealed off from the outside world, yet of course open to the sky.

Pools were segregated for centuries. Women-only pools still remain, like in Coogee, New South Wales. But today the pool is the place you see the bodies of everyone and anyone in all their glorious individualism. Scars, scratches, fat, ripples, muscle, curves, hair, skin of every tone. The human body is as idiosyncratic and imperfect as every doctor dispassionately knows it to be. And the experience is the complete opposite of consuming media where bodies are shown as extremes of heaven and hell rather than as a weltering array of everything and nothing. Spectators outnumbered swimmers at lidos in the first half of the 20th century. Like the beach, the pool was the only place save for the art gallery where you could see the population's bodies before society became saturated with selfies and porn.

Pools can be transgressive spaces too. Fashion often appeals to those most marginalized by the patriarchy – people who are queer, women, young people, people of colour; pools do too. Pools are not the places where middle-aged, middle-class men gather – they seem to prefer hobbies involving mecahnics and 0competition (so, okay, maybe you'll see them triathlon training). This leaves lidos as free spaces where you will witness teenagers flirting, old ladies gossiping, freelancers scribbling, and more pregnant women than you've ever encountered in your life. If to swim is to be reborn, then pregnant women upend the truism by getting in there early. Pools allow adults to act like kids and kids to act like adults. Leon Kossoff's paintings of pools in London show packed family fun days – they burst with vigour.

So, pools seem to be for everyone. But are they really? The lifeguards are from Colombia, the cleaners from Romania or the Philippines. The Welfare State in Europe was for the poor, but only the poor of rich countries who in the grand scheme of things were never doing that badly, with services staffed by those from former protectorates where the situation was worse. Public pools are only provided by governments in rich countries. Pools have been the site of racial conflict in Australia and the USA. In 1964 the manager of the Monson Motor Lodge in St Augustine, Florida, poured hydrochloric acid into the water when white and black students together staged an aquatic 'wade in', a watery tribute to Rosa Parks aimed at ending poolside segregation during the Civil Rights struggle. Swim Dem Crew and others have tried to mix things up more recently, to bring more swimmers of colour into the water in the UK.

In developing countries the situation is stark: 4 out of 5 of people can't swim, versus 1 in 5 in the developed world. We luxuriate in pools while in Dhaka, Lagos, Port Moresby, Port-au-Prince and all the rest there are scarcely any. Drownings in the poorest and wettest countries like Bangladesh are sky-high because swimming is not taught. For those of us lucky enough to live in the First World, memories of learning are rich: diving to pick up bricks (why?) and wearing pyjamas to the pool – because sleepwalkers can drown too, right? I still have no idea how I ended up learning to swim in a pool on an East Anglian RAF fighter base with

a full-size English Electric Lightning fighter aircraft poised on a plinth by the entrance, but the memory will never leave me.

For those of us lucky enough to possess a pool or live near one, the blissful experience of being in the water is almost transcendent on days when the sun lasers down, whether it's a bracing winter dip or a cooling summer one. The world looks so strange when it's full of reflections and refractions – the colours of the buildings and the birds and the aircraft and the sky all seem heightened. The rhythm of breathing and moving muscles takes you to a place beyond your usual self; the writer Joe Minihane makes a case for swimming as the ultimate mental health tool and after completing your lengths you'll be hard pushed to disagree with that sentiment. The underwater world is a parallel realm of dreams and distortion and bubbles that you can enjoy until your breath runs out. Filmmakers, writers and artists have long seen the creative potential in this magical world. The introduction of *Soy Cuba* – the greatest opening sequence of any movie – delivers its jazz-soundtracked coup de grace when the camera descends into the rooftop pool of the Hotel Capri in Havana and gives us a fish-eye view that blows you away. The swimming pool has starred in underrated Aubrey Plaza comedy *The To Do List*, the 1970 Jerzy Skolimowski thriller *Deep End* and Guillaume Brac's documentary *L'Île au trésor*.

Pools have inspired architects to produce great works – like North Sydney Olympic Pool by Rudder & Grout and Lucien Pollet's Piscine Molitor, though more often the architecture is understated. Artists like David Hockney and Ed Ruscha have seen the potential of pools too. In the out-of-print 2005 book *Liquid Assets*, Tracey Emin says she wants to design a chain of pools along the River Thames in London. 'They would be oval shaped, with an egg-like roof, which opens up when the sun comes out. And when that happened all the radio stations in London would make an announcement: "The London Ovals are opening!"'

Whether we care to admit it or not, a pool is a status symbol for an individual, a property developer, a hotel or a municipality. The pool as an Instagram sightbite is the predictable end result of this slippery process, the influencer as floating fodder for their own dreams of fame and fortune, their inflatable compatriot a unicorn or giant pizza slice. The infinity pool is the Patrick Bateman of swimming pools; the riad splash bath, the rooftop hot tub, the hotel horizon-chaser – images of instant gratification in our superficial, superfast world that ended up exactly as grubbily atomized as Ballard predicted it would. The pool on top of that oversized ironing table, the Marina Bay Sands in Singapore, is a bloated, bilious extravagance that can surely only be rivalled by a hovering pool held up by hot air balloons or a hundred drones.

The danger is that pools become a joke in the way that the High Line's imitators like London's Garden Bridge have done. Pools without access depicted in ridiculous renderings grafted to the top of skyscrapers, or skypools that link ugly residential blocks whose apartments are solely purchased off-plan by buyers in Kuala Lumpur or Shanghai, or pools that project above the traffic at 20 storeys and invite you to look down on your less fortunate brethren like you're the king of the castle. It's not so much the architects – they just take the money like teenagers when a parent's wallet is opened, it's their job – it's the developers who really embody the crassness of the age. You are left wondering – is it still the 1980s? But then the pool is a place of smugness, it always has been, because you're not doing any work as you front crawl in the sunshine, leaving your cares behind.

More shuttered lidos are reopening, new pools are arriving, more swimmers are discovering the joys of outdoor lengths. Floating pools in rivers and harbours and natural, chemical-free pools are the next big thing. A swimming pool renaissance is underway. Now it's not just the swimmer who is reborn but the pool itself. The old soldiers that have stood through the decades are now being appreciated in film and on the page. The lidos that have simply provided a community service are getting their dues. When every job is automated, the answer is this: to spend every day in this rhythm: swim, sweat, shower, dry, laze, watch, think, eat, sunbathe, relax. The lido today is a place of peace in a frenetic world that is going very slowly round the twist, an easy exercise option, a slice of concrete deck on which to observe the changing seasons and the differing angles of the sun, the ways the leaves on the trees turn from green to brown, to realize how life sloshes around and stubbornly refuses to let you fully control it, how each length and each morning brings you closer to death yet makes you feel so alive as you hurtle inextricably towards your final destination, one kick at a time.

EUROPE

NATURBAD
RIEHEN

Basel, Switzerland

Stroll out from Basel into the fields and
eventually you'll reach Naturbad Riehen,
which is tucked just inside Switzerland – or is
it Germany? The border swivels and switches
so much it's hard to tell which side you're
on. They speak the same language and the
countryside looks the same (as do the cows).
Riehen gets to grips with the latest hot topic in
swimming – natural pools. Free from chlorine
and instead cleaned by reeds and plants, it
resembles a rather pleasant pond. There's
attractive grass fringing it, on which kids mess
about. Then curving like a cuddle around
the outer perimeter is an innovative wooden
superstructure, including changing rooms
and café by Swiss starchitects Herzog & de
Meuron, with seating facing the pool and bike
racks all along the outside.

ISLANDS BRYGGE HAVNEBADET

Copenhagen, Denmark

Before Bjarke Ingels became more well known for his commercial work, he designed a pool. Out on the waterside in Copenhagen, along the old Icelandic quayside (fun fact: Iceland was a part of Denmark until 1944), you can find this free-wheeling, jolly little 2003 endeavour from Bjarke, along with his Belgian friend Julien De Smedt. There's a red and white stripy tower which looks more like the radar stations you see at the end of Spanish airport runways than a lighthouse (which I think it's supposed to evoke), but who cares? The wooden superstructure and its weird angles encourage all that come to dive in. Copenhagen is very keen on its outdoor swims and there are many opportunities for a dip elsewhere too: the Bavnehøj and Bellahøj pools on social housing estates built with the utmost respect for their residents, and the Kastrup Sea Bath poised out over the Baltic – nicknamed the 'Snail' and built in wood by White Arkitekter in 2005.

BAINS DES PÂQUIS

Geneva, Switzerland

An interesting example of a campaign to save a lido occurred here in Geneva in the 1980s, the decade that was the darkest for our pools. More pools closed around the world during this period than at any other point – mainly due to them reaching old age and needing expensive repairs, coupled with a huge drop in usage which tallied with new indoor leisure centres opening and a drastic drop in package holiday prices to sunnier climes. So to Geneva where the 1870s Bains des Pâquis (rebuilt in the Streamline Moderne style in the 1930s) were threatened. A fantastic Tin Tin-style poster by cartoonist Emmanuel Excoffier (alias Exem) depicted a giant, Manga-esque octopus emerging from Lac Léman and ripping up the famous diving boards of this lakeside lido on its own promontory, which is a historic part of Geneva's lakefront. In the end the battle was won: the heritage pools and piers were restored and have eventually become very well patronized once more.

24

PISCINE DU RHÔNE

Lyon, France

The Rhône and the Saône both slither through Lyon, France's elegant third city, before meeting at the Confluence – once one of Europe's busiest inland ports. The riverbanks have been under renewal for decades. The latest schemes include art galleries, offices and a huge museum. But this earlier attempt to bring the Lyonnais back to their riverfront dates from 1968. The former Piscine du Rhône (now the Centre Nautique Tony Bertrand) is big (the French love a *Grand Projet* after all), stretching for what seems like half a kilometre along a prime stretch of waterfront in the city centre, that in more money-minded nations would have been carved up, sold off and coated in depressing real estate. Not here. A gutsy multi-pool complex is enhanced with tanning terraces and cafés, slides and fountains. The symbols of the place are the thrusting pylons that reach up into the sky and illuminate everything below at dusk. A long repair job in the 2010s brought the place back to its former glory.

ZOLLVEREIN
MINE POOL

Essen, Germany

An interesting lesson in industry and memory lies in wait in the Ruhr. Compare Britain to Germany and the former falls flat over and over again – Britain's coal mines were eradicated. In Germany the pride that went into these places has never gone away and they have been preserved in some style. Zollverein is memorialized in a kind of post-apocalyptic park, where you can stroll through industrial remains and over slag heaps planted with trees, crossing once-busy railway tracks and admiring the dinosaur-like machinery and robust architecture of the coal sorting complex by Martin Kremmer and Fritz Schrupp, two students of Walter Gropius, from the 1930s. Various conspiracy theories fly around about why it wasn't blown up in the Second World War, some say American shareholders strong-armed the allies into deliberately not bombing it. Today schoolkids are taught about the Ruhr's past at this UNESCO World Heritage Site and at the centre, next to the coke processing room, is a pool from 2001 by Frankfurt artists Dirk Paschke and Daniel Milohnic where you can swim surrounded by the ghastly, ghostly and ultimately uplifting remains of blast furnaces and so much metal pipework. It is art, sport and memory all mixed together. The pool is small but perfectly formed; Zollverein itself is sprawling and unforgettable.

PISCINA MUNICIPAL DE MONTJUÏC

Barcelona, Spain

Of the all the most magnificent homages to Catalonia, this is certainly the most democratic, and for that at least George Orwell, that great describer of the chaos of 1930s Barcelona, would be proud. One wonders what he'd make of Catalonia's current political upheavals and of the fact that the Sagrada Familia, which protrudes noticeably from the skyline when viewed from up here, is still not complete. The pool was dug out before Orwell arrived – these days it looks scruffy enough to have dated from those times, despite being remodelled several times for the Mediterranean Games in 1955 and of course the 1992 Olympics, the greatest Olympiad ever and the one in which architecture made its mark and Spain made its return from the fascist wilderness it entered in the 1930s. The televised shots of the divers with the city behind them mesmerized many who have never visited. Those that have revel in the location atop the city's mountain and ignore the leaks and the flaking paint.

BLUE LAGOON

Iceland

The first or last stop for many tourists because it's on the road from Reykjavik to the former NATO base and now Iceland's international airport at Keflavik, the Blue Lagoon is Disney does geology. A polished, primped, scrupulously cleaned experience at odds with the fire and the muck below, the Blue Lagoon is a modern spa set around the ancient workings of the Earth. To wit: you can swim in warm waters heated by magma on even the coldest and darkest January morning on this bizarre island. There's more paddling, selfies and cocktails than actual swimming but it's a diverting lesson in how what lies beneath our feet is not boring, not constant, not simple, but full of power and drama.

FREIBAD MIRKE

Wuppertal, Germany

The main reason people visit Wuppertal is to ride its amazingly anachronistic Schwebebahn – or hanging railway – which sails above the roofs and the river Wupper. But actually this post-industrial city is something of a mini Berlin in west Germany – a low-key hipster town populated by DJs and designers where rents cost peanuts and culture is central to life. Ergo Freibad Mirke, one of the city's original public pools and in fact one of the oldest in Germany, dating from 1851, has been the focus of a concerted community effort to get it back on track and open in recent years. Art, music and events have been staged in the bucolic grounds of the former 'people's pool', by a group of charming locals, including music journalist Csilla Letay. Parties in the new pool are a fixture of the summer season, organic gardening takes place in the grounds and family picnics are common: all of them make this a wonderful example of how to bring a faded pool back from the dead. They've currently got a 'pool within a pool' up and running but want to restore the entire pool as a natural, chemical-free concern.

ZELENÁ ŽABA

Slovakia

Czech architect Bohuslav Fuchs was a little known but important force in the functionalist movement that brought a freshness and robustness to modernism in the 1930s. He developed a bit of a tendency towards swimming pools, working on the Zábrdovice baths in his adopted home city of Brno, and then the famed Zelená Žaba complex (it means 'green frog' – isn't that loveable?) in the hills to the east of Tren in what is – since the Velvet Divorce – Slovakia. Set in a spa resort, Zelená Žaba's spiral staircases and ample use of reds and yellows have a little in common with Lubetkin or Corbusier's oeuvre, and the changing room block peering down the hill at the pool is as pretty as a picture. It was renovated in 2015 – restoring some original features but also aggressively modernizing others.

ALLAS SEA POOL

Helsinki, Finland

Swimming on a ship or swimming while you can see ships adds a pleasant, piquant touch to an al fresco dip. You get the feeling you're doing the former at Helsinki's harbour pool, because the whole set-up is floating on top of the chilly Baltic. And there's no doubt about the latter because absolutely enormous ferries start their engines, spin around and chug off right in front of you, bound for Stockholm. Apparently the entertainment on board is quite amusing (though you'll find most Finns at the bar). And swimming here is a lark too. As well as the ships you can run your eye over Helsinki's distinctly Russian-looking waterfront buildings like the City Hall and Cathedral. This new addition to the harbour by architects Huttunen-Lipasti-Pakkanen is mostly in wood and also has a sauna where you can warm up after your swim. If you're wondering about swimming in the Baltic then wonder no longer: I've done it and it's absolutely freezing. If that's your bag, take a sauna at Löyly and you can dive straight into the sea – but it's not for the faint of heart.

BADESCHIFF

Berlin, Germany

Swimming in Berlin has not always been fun. It could be deadly serious. On the 5 October 1961, sick of the malaise of living in the East, Udo Düllick tried to swim the Spree river and escape to freedom. Düllick quietly entered the water on the north bank, not far from the piles of the landmark Oberbaumbrücke. East German border guards were instructed to shoot at anyone suspected of *Republikflucht* (escaping the country) and when they spied him they opened up. They missed Düllick but tragedy struck and he drowned before he could reach the other side. The same fate robbed five more DDR citizens of their lives in the same place, a further five were shot dead by the border guards on nights when their aim was better (fewer glasses of Radeberger?). A few hundred metres from this point, partygoers at Badeschiff barely even know this story. Today's Berlin runs on fun not fear. The 'bathing ship' (well, more of a barge) is towed back to its position by the Arena Club every spring, and the floating pool thrums with squeals, the clinking of glasses and pounding techno music.

PISCINA DAS MARÉS

Porto, Portugal

Where does the man-made end and the natural begin? That's the question you're left asking yourself at Álvaro Siza's celebrated sea pools, the *Poços de Marés de Leça da Palmeira*. The Portuguese architect has done nothing less than imagine how nature might have built its own tidal swimming pool if the sea somehow had a consciousness and could choose where its waves broke and the shapes that it wanted to erode. It really looks as if the sea does have brains and did indeed make these pools outside Porto as some sort of bet with the sky. In reality Siza spent the 1960s building these pools – one of his first built projects – and tacking on stylishly minimalist changing rooms. The pools became derelict around 2004, but since receiving a heritage listing from the Portuguese government in 2012, they have been restored and are once again drawing in swimmers with a taste for the eccentric.

PISCINE
MOLITOR

Paris, France

The Piscine Molitor has been recently
refurbished and is now part of the Sofitel/
MGallery branded Hotel Molitor. This
revolutionary al fresco pool was where the
singers, dancers, prancers and chancers of
the jazz age took the plunge into perfect
waters. Despite its early popularity with the
cognoscenti, it fell on tough times as its life
went on, becoming almost a wreck and was
nearly bulldozed in the 1980s. It stood idle
and ruined for many years until its recent
rescue and resuscitation. Designed by Lucien
Pollet in 1929, its typically art deco lines
evoked ocean liners and luxury, as well as
freshness, health and decadence – the bikini
was debuted here in 1946 and the world
never looked back (though it did look over its
shoulder rather a lot).

LAKE BLED LIDO

Slovenia

The cute couples who stroll the lake shore remind you that so often you take the best relationships for granted – never fully realizing what you had until you've lost it. Slovenia needs to make sure it treasures Lake Bled, and doesn't push it too much by trying to capitalize on the shoreline with hotels or conference centres, built to attract global elites. Because this lake is stunning – topped by a teetering castle, it even includes an island you can swim out to. An easier way to enjoy the waters is at the lido on the western side. The waters are enclosed and there are sundecks and diving boards. The long-time lifeguard who runs the show looks like an ageing David Hasselhoff-wannabe with grey chest hair and a predilection for shouting out insults and jokes in English.

OLYMPIA SCHWIMM-STADION

Berlin, Germany

The idea that politics can be kept out of sport is laughable – sport is pure politics. The 1936 Olympics in Berlin demonstrated that perhaps more than any other sporting event. Luckily Jesse Owens' victory on the track and Dorothy Poynton-Hill's dives from the high board into the pool made more waves, literally and metaphorically, than Hitler's disgraceful theatrics. The Schwimmstadion, the work of Werner March, is as overblown and frankly terrifying as the Olympiastadion it abuts. Coated in limestone, it forms the northern axis of the sprawing Olympic site, and boasts ceramic reliefs by Max Laeuger and landscaping by Heinrich Wiepking-Jürgensmann. It is a strange place perhaps for a summer swim, but as with Tempelhof Airport, Berlin has decided to make the best of a past that went horribly wrong and instead provide a place where locals – like those living next door in Corbusier's lesser-known copy of the Unité d'Habitation in Marseille – can cool off.

HALUDOVO HOTEL

Krk, Croatia

Believe it or not, *Penthouse* magazine brought capitalism behind the Iron Curtain when they bizarrely teamed up with the Yugoslavs to launch this state-of-the-art hotel in the late 1960s, crowned with a lavish pool complex. Though maybe it wasn't so far-fetched – for centuries hard Western currency has been treasured by states that, for whatever reason, haven't had the wherewithal to generate it through their own economies. So it was on the Croatian island of Krk. The Dalmatian coast was undergoing a tourism boom at that time, and still is today. Odd, then, that this landmark hotel has fallen into disrepair. The spectacular concrete gutters and brutalist lines by Boris Magaš remain. Who will come and restore this pool and the hotel that surrounds it?

ALT-ERLAA ROOFTOP POOLS

Vienna, Austria

The received wisdom on public housing estates has always been that their success lies in the facilities and the surroundings as much as the apartments. And that does seem to ring true. The isolated, grey Plattenbau blocks that sit on windswept, unkempt ground with nary a minimart don't seem to do as well as the thoughtfully planned schemes that included things residents needed and attempted to make a community: people need shops, doctors' surgeries and public transport. Vienna has a reputation for being bourgeois (which it is in some ways), but its housing programme for the last hundred years has been fiercely progressive. One such example at the fringes of the city is Alt-Erlaa, by architect Harry Glück. With its own U-Bahn stop, library, local paper, landscaping and schools it seems very liveable. The imposing housing superblocks are monumental and the public art in the lobbies is often rather stark. But the rooftops are where it's at. Each block has a swimming pool in the sky for residents. Not just a paddling pool for the kids after Le Corbusier's Unité d'Habitation, but a full swimming pool for easy morning exercise. The views back over Vienna are enough to lift the heart too. One wonders how different things might have been for the many similar demolished blocks of Europe and the USA if they'd all had such watery treasures on their roofs.

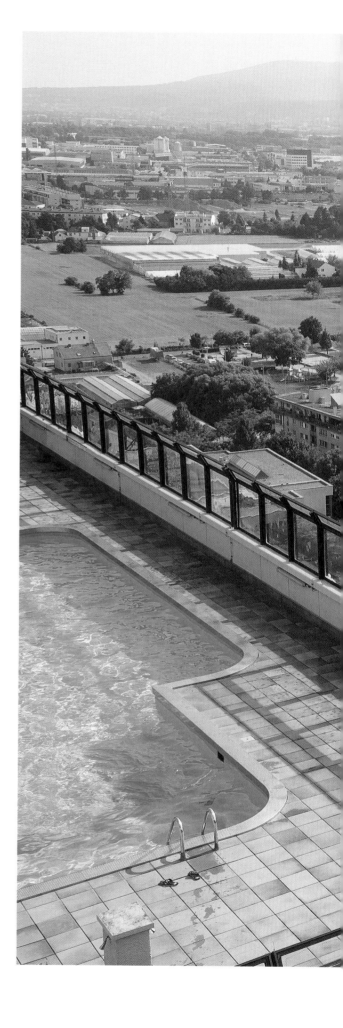

LIDO DI MILANO

Milan, Italy

The fascist-era architecture of the main al fresco pool in Milan – in the San Siro district near the city's famous football stadium – offers a stark welcome. There is a long, curved entrance barrier with grumpy friezes curving round columns depicting gods, monsters and sea serpents. Puts you right in the mood for a swim. The huge complex inside includes a massive pool with an island and a circular pavilion watching over things from one end. Cesare Marescotti's original 1931 design included moorings and a bridge, but these were removed. You can also play beach volleyball here. And it's worth noting of course the British use of 'lido' comes from the Italian for beach – interesting to see though that the Italians were also using it to refer to a pool as a kind of 'urban beach'. Italy has lots of coast but hardly any Italian city – especially not Milan – is actually by the sea with its own beaches. This is why the sweltering citizens of Rome, Bologna, Verona, Pisa and Turin value their annual trip to Positano or Rimini, or their afternoon at the city lido, so much.

SEEBAD UTOQUAI

Zurich, Switzerland

Zurich's lake baths fulfil the typically Swiss need for something that feels as close to a beach and as close to the sea as you'll get in a landlocked country. Almost every city in the country has something along these lines. But being landlocked is not the problem we often think it is. Find me someone who'd take a cold, wet weekend in a British coastal village over a sunny day on Lake Zurich, where the temperature of the water may even be warmer than that of some sea resorts. Utoquai is a charming affair anyway – historic bathing buildings clustered hard against the water's edge and plenty of swimmers taking a dip just five minutes from the centre of Switzerland's largest city. An added attraction for architecture fans is the Pavilion Le Corbusier, the Swiss architect's final work, completed posthumously in 1967 and just a short stroll from Utoquai. It was restored and reopened in 2019, following several wilderness years of sad dereliction.

Libby Page

Novelist
Author of *The Lido*

What do you like about lidos?

Lidos are very special places. They are places where people come together to enjoy a simple pleasure – swimming in the open air. Teenagers hanging out in the summer, families with young children, people training for triathlons or simply enjoying a few lengths for their mental health. There's something about stripping down to your swimsuit that is a great unifier. For city dwellers like me, swimming beneath the sky is a connection to nature and the outdoors – there is something very special about watching birds fly overhead and feeling the breeze on your face as you swim. Lots of lidos are also really special architecturally – that squat brick art deco-type building is so iconic. Lidos feel like a real part of our heritage in the UK, even more precious now that so many have sadly closed. They are hubs of the community, links to the past and places worth fighting for.

What inspired you to write *The Lido*?

I lived in Brixton as a student, not far from the beautiful Brockwell Lido. As a recent newcomer to London, I was struggling to find my place in the city and to find a sense of community. But at the lido I saw people of all backgrounds chatting in the changing rooms and on the poolside. It made me think about these places within our communities where people can make real connections with one another, and how much we lose when these places, be they lidos, libraries or independent bookshops, close down.

Where did the characters and story come from?

My book is fictional, but some of the characters were inspired by lido regulars. Rosemary's character in particular (the 86-year-old who has swum at the lido all her life) was inspired by the older women you so often see at a lido who brave the chilly water when teenagers are shivering on the side – I love that bravery and sense of energy.

Do you like swimming? Why?

Imagine if I said no! I love swimming. Funnily though, I was never a very confident swimmer when I was younger and went through many years of not swimming at all. I felt self-conscious and anxious out of my depth. But in my first job after university a colleague went swimming every morning before work and swore by the mental health benefits. So I decided to go with her. I was terrible at first but very quickly found she was right – I found it really relaxing and meditative. My older sister (who is a strong swimmer) gave me a few lessons and over a year or so I worked on improving my stroke until I became a confident swimmer and felt able to go from indoor pools, to lidos, to lakes, rivers and the sea.

London Fields is my local lido. Which is yours?

I had the inspiration for my book while living a short walk from Brockwell Lido, but I have since moved to north-east London so London Fields is actually my local now too. I am building up to swimming all year in cold water (I enjoy swimming at Parliament Hill lido, which is unheated, as well as the Ladies Pond in Hampstead) but in the meantime I must admit I enjoy the fact that London Fields is heated! I enjoy the fact I don't have to stop swimming even during the coldest spells in the winter. I just have to brave a quick dash to the water but once inside it is warm. I love that contrast in sensations – the cold air and the warm water. From a practical reason I love that I'm able to cycle to London Fields Lido from my flat. I often go there in the morning, swim, and then do some writing in a nearby café afterwards.

What did you learn from writing *The Lido*?

Writing the book has changed my life. I'm now lucky enough to be a full-time writer, and the whole process of getting the book published and adapting to life as an author has been a huge learning experience for me. It has also furthered my love of lidos and made me want to seek out more to swim in.

Which other lidos do you like?

There are so many lidos across the country that I would still love to visit – I need to do a road trip like the authors of *The Lido Guide* (a comprehensive guide to the UK's outdoor pools). In London, I love Brockwell, of course, as well as Tooting and Charlton. I've also swum in Cheltenham's lido and the lovely little lido in Petersfield. I actually learnt to swim at an outdoor pool – the very small but very lovely Tisbury pool. I remember the water being freezing, although I believe it is heated now.

Why are lidos interesting for writers?

I was drawn to setting my book at a lido because they are real community hubs and places where all sorts of characters can interact and stories can take place. But there are so many things about lidos that appeal as a writer. They are very visually exciting places – that vibrant blue, the light on the water, the changing weather overhead.

UNITED KINGDOM

LONDON FIELDS LIDO

Hackney, London

I don't mind admitting that I was apprehensive the first time I plunged in here, encouraged by a person who still remains very special to me and who always will. But how quickly reticence turns to obsession. Nowadays, you can find this overthinking writer doing laps here pretty much every day he's in London – look for the idiot in pink shorts and sunnies and feel free to come and say hi. London Fields has something of a reputation as Britain's most hipster lido and there is some truth in that – on weekday afternoons it's more like WeWork-on-Sea with creative and tech freelancers blathering away on their phones and plenty of good-looking, well-groomed types. On warm weekends it gets hot 'n' hectic with locals and inebriated Hackney house-sharers in their twenties. But the heated pool is perfect year round and winter sees hardened triathletes take over, along with older swimmers whose bodies prove that a daily dip is probably the single best choice you can make in life if you want to live a little longer. This ultimately modest (and incredibly well-managed and maintained) lido exists – save from the cute coloured changing room doors – without fanfare and was the work of Harry Arnold Rowbotham and T. L. Smithson from London County Council's Parks Department. It opened in 1932 and had a twin in Kennington Park, which bit the dust in 1987. It has been refurbished several times and is now one of the city's most endearing little pockets of calm and pleasure.

Why I Swim

Renay Richardson
London

Why do you love to swim?
Swimming is my escape, it's where I can completely relax and be in 'the zone'. I see people swimming with earphones but I just love popping in my earplugs and blocking out the world.

What is it about lidos and outdoor pools in particular that appeals?
I live in Hackney so London Fields is my lido of choice. I did go to the Hampstead Ponds for the first time last summer so will definitely be doing that again.

Which ones do you especially like?
This sounds so fancy, but I was in Canggu on the island of Bali in Indonesia earlier this year, and there was a local lido I went to every morning I was there that cost about 50p a pop. I was there as soon as it opened and got my 40-50 lengths in. It was awesome. It wasn't upmarket or anything but just having a pool to yourself is bliss. That place would be my secret tip. The Taman Rekreasi Marina Pool.

How does swimming make you feel?
Swimming is freedom, whether it's in a pool or in the sea, a lake or a pond. It's one of my favourite things to do. I learned to swim in 2016, it was the best thing I've ever done.

BRISTOL LIDO

Bristol

Here we have an interesting experiment in what a lido can become. Gentrified beyond belief, the Bristol Lido in the Clifton area of the city now boasts a spa, poolside bar and high-end restaurant, which serves food 'in the spirit of hedonism rather than health'. High-quality finishes, clever branding and a natty website complete the transformation – and it reminds me somewhat of what the Germans do with their tired old pools to make them rather more attractive, like at Neptunbad in Cologne and Oderberger in Berlin – both historic former *stadtbad* that have been thoroughly modernized. At Clifton the Grade II* listed lido from way back in 1850 had been closed for years. The same company that took on Clifton's lido went on to restore the one in Reading, too.

SALTDEAN LIDO

Brighton

The modernism of England's south coast is not always noted, seldom even noticed. Yet it did offer a shot in the arm to several fading Edwardian resorts, with examples such as Deal Pier, Bottle Alley in St Leonards, the art deco Embassy Court by Wells Coates in Brighton, and Serge Chermayeff and Erich Mendelsohn's symphony to smoothness, the De La Warr Pavilion in Bexhill, which has something in common with Saltdean's lustrous lido – probably England's best looking, though should we judge lidos on their personality too these days? With its embracing arms and symmetrical purity it speaks so parlously of the age of health, efficiency and the new, an age that was interrupted by war and only really resumed again in the 1960s. Saltdean's story is also one of a committed community who saved this gem from the wrecking ball (how could they even think of that?) and slowly restored it once more to its glory in our second age of swimming. The original architect was R. W. H. Jones.

Why I Swim

Deborah Arthurs
Richmond, Surrey, UK

Why do you love to swim?

Swimming always feels so meditative and cleansing. Sometimes it takes sheer willpower to get to the pool and jump in, but I never regret going. While I swim, there can be no other distractions. It's one of the only times in my life I don't have my phone in my hand (I know – this is bad). But it means I totally switch off from distractions. When I'm focusing on my breathing and my stroke, all that's in my mind is that – and as my body gets used to the cold, to the breathing, I find my rhythm; I feel so energized, like I could swim forever. Outdoor swimming – particularly in a wild swimming spot or large pool – feels different too. You are swimming in much colder water than usual and there are waves to contend with. It's so invigorating.

What is it about lidos and outdoor pools in particular that appeals?

Swimming in the open air is so special. There is no smell of chlorine. None of that echoey, shouty clatter of an indoor pool. Lidos and outdoor pools are quite and calm, especially if you go before work. There is nothing like a 7am swim in the lido to wake you up and make you feel like an absolute champ.

Which ones do you especially like?

As I live in Richmond, I usually swim in the outdoor pool at the Old Deer Park. It has been part of the Richmond community for years, and friends who grew up in the area remember spending summer holidays there when they were kids. Now the big slide has gone, but it's still surrounded by lawns and there are palm trees lining the pool, so as you swim backstroke, you just look up at the blue skies (if you're lucky) and palm fronds. You could really be anywhere. It's the ultimate escapism.

My other favourite is the lido at Walpole Bay, Cliftonville, in Margate (which a group of investors is looking to buy and restore). I swim there every time I go, between say March and November. Usually I don't wear a wetsuit, though in the colder months if anyone else dares to brave the cold, most do wear wetsuits. Margate Lido is truly lovely. Huge – probably three swimming pool lengths across – and refreshed every tide. The concrete sides are covered in moss and rusty metal stairs lead into the water, though I always, always just jump straight in with a big scream. When the tide rushes in over the sides you can swim against it. If the weather is harsh, it's choppy and browny-green. When it's sunny, it is mirror-smooth and gleaming. On those days it could be the Caribbean (honest – I have pics!). You get all sorts of sea birds on the sides and joining you in the water, and at sunset when the water is tinged pink, the birds circle above. It's a stunner.

The Oasis in Covent Garden I loved when I was a student. An outdoor swimming pool, surrounded by buildings rising up from its sides, right in the centre of London. Loved it. And it was inexpensive and public. I also like Brockwell Lido, which I have swum in many times, though not for years, and Hampstead Ponds, if that counts. The lidos in Sydney are lovely. Sitting at the bar at Bondi Beach Icebergs Club overlooking the pool below is magical.

Any lido advice?

Yes, telling people not to leave their shoes and clothes on the walls at the side of Margate Lido. You think they are safe – then *whoosh!* The tide comes in and before you know it, all your things have gone and you're walking home in your cossie.

TINSIDE LIDO

Plymouth

John Wibberley's masterwork is a lido the
city of Plymouth can truly be proud of. The
enormous curved pool projects out into the
English Channel below the famous Hoe where
Francis Drake liked a game of bowls and a
smoke on his pipe, as every English school
child will know. Anyway this huge lido has
an eight-sided theme – octagonal fountains
at either corner and one in the middle
bring the whole piece to life. Completed in
1935, it succumbed like so many others to a
closure (1992–2005), which would be totally
unthinkable today. Tinside is also listed at
Grade II, making it one of the most important
pieces of modern architecture in the country
from that period, up there with the likes of the
Lawn Road Flats in Hampstead, North London,
opened the year before.

PARLIAMENT HILL LIDO

Hampstead, London

Pools can be both elitist and democratic spaces, like so much in architecture. The private pool is a symbol of indulgence, the public a gift to everyone. Parliament Hill reminds us very definitely which category it falls into with the vintage newspaper clippings from its opening in 1938. They proudly announce that this watery wonder is available to working people for just a few pence, and with no membership requirements. Set at the foot of Parliament Hill, just before it rises into Hampstead Heath, this is the Pavarotti of lidos – big, but not perhaps big enough for its fans. Queueing barriers go up in summer out the front, making you think you're waiting for the newest rollercoaster at a theme park. The interiors are showing their age but there is so much space and light outside. This is heightened by the unusual metallic lining of the unheated pool.

Why I Swim

Rebecca Armstrong
London, UK

Why do you love to swim?

Swimming calms my mind – as soon as I walk onto the terrace
of Parliament Hill Lido, my shoulders drop and I relax. I feel like
the water absorbs my woes, that it washes away my worries and
leaves me mentally refreshed. I tag all of the pictures that I post on
Instagram of my swimming with #mentalhealth because I feel like it
has saved my sanity. It's also satisfying, as someone who isn't very
fit, to use my body and for it to do me proud. I suppose I'd say that
swimming helps me body and soul.

What is it about lidos and outdoor pools in particular that appeals?

The sky! Seeing the light change as I swim, seeing birds flying
overhead or – on great days at the lido – the ducks swimming in the
pool with me, and the crows having a drink from the water. I love how
the view changes through the year, from the bony fingers of winter
trees visible with lost kites in their clutches, to the rose-gold late
afternoon sun spilling across the water in the summer.

Do you have any favourite pools?

I love Parliament Hill Lido for its size, its shimmering metal lining and
because it's so close to where I live. The atmosphere is wonderful, as
is that at the Ladies' Pond on Hampstead Heath. The lido has a café
and, in the winter, a sauna, which makes swimming in two-degree

water much more palatable, but the relative wildness of the pond is a special kind of magic, even if it doesn't have hot chocolate on tap. I also swim in the Walpole Bay tidal pool in Margate when I visit friends. I feel very safe in the water there and it has all the benefits of the sea without, for me, the fear factor. I'm not keen on the occasional jellyfish bobbing by, but it's where my friend Anna introduced me to the joys of cold-water swimming so it will always be precious to me.

Do you especially like the architecture of any lidos?

I love the art deco lines and curves of Parliament Hill and Tooting Bec. The changing rooms in Parliament Hill Lido are hilariously old school, but I'm very fond of them and would be put out if they had a swanky facelift. I remember going to the lido in Swindon as a child and I was horrified and fascinated in equal measure by the fact that the deep end was in the middle. The grandeur of a good 1930s lido is so heartwarming – the fact that these vast places were built for everybody to enjoy in a stately style makes me feel a little bit tearful.

Where do you swim and how often?

My regular haunts are Parliament Hill and the Ponds. I swam all last winter, going two or three times a week. The lido is easier for me to get to from home and work, so that rather pips the Ponds, but in summer I might swim up to five times a week, either before work or after it.

How does swimming make you feel?

More sane, more serene and just so happy. I love that I can go for a swim and be among people even if I don't necessarily socialize. I've made friends going who are very precious to me, but even if I don't see anyone I know, I never feel lonely. I recently swam in the Danube on a trip to Vienna, and had a dip in front of the Belém Tower in Lisbon. I try and keep a swimming costume and my microfibre towel in my bag at all times in case I find some water to get acquainted with.

Any anecdotes from being at the lido?

I took part in an ice swim in January. I didn't realize it was a race and – given that I swim like an old lady doing head-out-of-the-water breaststroke – was mortified at the thought of being so slow. I cried, and nearly didn't take part. But I did it, laughing like a mad woman, and brought up the rear.

HAMPSTEAD HEATH PONDS

Hampstead, London

Londoners love Hampstead Heath because they can pretend – if only for a little while – that they are living in the countryside. George Orwell often walked up here when he lived at 77 Parliament Hill and just past his house is the Parliament Hill summit from which you can survey the whole glorious, riotous, ruinous city in full. This is a perfect place for contemplation or proposals. And if you keep walking you get to the Mixed Bathing Pond. It is ludicrously oversubscribed in summer but the cool, crisp water is heaven-sent when it's hot and the raucous atmosphere is diverting. Over on the east side of the Heath you can find the Highgate Men's Pond and the Kenwood Ladies' Pond. These are both quieter affairs and spark more love among their users than the busy mixed pond. The Ponds were dug as reservoirs for drinking water and are for many people their first (safe) taste of the kind of wild swimming Joe Minihane and Roger Deakin advocate in their respective books, *Floating* and *Waterlog*. A documentary film, *The Ponds*, from Patrick McLennan and Samuel Smith, was released in 2019 showing a year in the life of the Ponds' swimmers – gasp as you watch these hardy souls swimming under the ice in winter from the comfort of your cinema seat.

STONEHAVEN HEATED OPEN AIR POOL

Aberdeenshire, Scotland

On May 25 2019 Britain's most northerly lido opened for the start of its eighty-fifth season. One of the bathers who was here in 1934 was still around but she couldn't make it from the old folks' home. But the great grandson of Olympic champions Elenor and Ken McKay, who both swam at 'Stoney', was here. Pete, Dave, Wendy and the rest of the 'friends' handed out bottles of Irn Bru and snacks and showed me press cuttings about bathing beauties contests and pipe repairs. A vote was held in Stonehaven in 1933 about building this perfect place, with 660 yesses and 539 nos. One can tell how much this pool means to everyone in the town today though – they had to fight to keep it open in the 1990s and it felt like Libby Page's novel *The Lido* come to life, which, weirdly, I'd been reading on the train down. The water was as warm as a bath. You'd love it. Jump in.

Why I Swim

Pete Hill
Aberdeenshire, Scotland

Why do you love to swim?

I was never much good as a footballer or at running as a kid, unlike most of my friends, and was usually one of the last ones to get picked when sides were being selected for a kick-about. Swimming was different though. I went for Sunday morning lessons at one of the old pools in Birmingham (Woodcock Street Baths with Mrs E. Jones officiating) and steadily progressed through the different levels, earning badges and reaching a standard where, for once, I was the best, fastest and most-accomplished among my mates, and it was a nice feeling. You can't unlearn how to swim and even now, what I learnt over 50 years ago, still means that I can go down the length of a pool at a reasonable speed. Even having the water-confidence to just float around doing nothing appeals. Swimming also got me first into snorkelling and subsequently scuba diving – two other activities that I have enjoyed for many years.

What is it about lidos and outdoor pools in particular that appeals?

Swimming in the sea is one thing but Birmingham is over 80km (50 miles) in any direction from the nearest sea water and Dad didn't have a car. The visit to the seaside was a once-a-year event but fortunately the 'new' baths at Stechford had an outside pool. It was lots of fun coming outside from the main pool braving the cold air to jump into the steaming water. It was a novelty doing the same when it was bucketing it down with rain, something I still enjoy to this day – usually you get the pool to yourself. I've never understood this aversion some people have to using a lido in the rain – you're going to get wet in any case, where's the problem?

Which lidos particularly appeal to you?

Stechford was my first but Street (Somerset) during the long, hot summer of 1976 brings back many happy memories. I've visited the Portishead Lido when down for a lido conference and also the tidally-filled Clevedon Marine Lake. As a geophysicist in the oil industry for over 35 years, I've also got a yearning for geothermally-heated pools. The Blue Baths in Rotorua, New Zealand, are superb. My wife and I were the only ones in there on a winter's day a few years ago – the main pool was very warm but the side pools were hot! The baths were built at the same time as the Stonehaven Pool in Scotland – the lido-building craze went on all over the Anglo-sphere. Iceland is great too – the Blue Lagoon is the only place where I've been able to get a beer and a swim at the same time, but the smaller (cheaper) municipal pools are not to be missed either. Pool complexes like the one in Bad Schandau in Germany are also not to be missed – interconnected indoor and outdoor pools, flumes and wave machines and the opportunity to strip off completely and use the saunas and steam rooms upstairs.

Do you enjoy the architecture of any lidos?

The 1930s was the time of the rise of the lidos and I love the art deco style which was used so much in the buildings at the time. Stonehaven, Portishead and Rotorua are really good examples.

Where do you swim and how often?

Mainly in Stonehaven and not enough! Since retiring I don't make enough time for myself to go swimming. In all honesty, being the Chairman of the Friends of Stonehaven Open Air Pool means that I'm usually fretting about the place and frequently a trip to the pool is accompanied by the occasional ear-bashing about something not working or that needs doing!

HATHERSAGE SWIMMING POOL

Derbyshire

It is February in England. A drab winter weekday in Derbyshire, the rain lashes down. The isolation and depressing qualities of rural life that are seldom noted by high-spirited summer trippers from the cities are only exacerbated by the cold. Who would swim on such a morning? And yet... could there be anything more heartening (apart from a hot Cornish pasty from the nearby bakery) than a dip in this charming little pool. Which, incredibly, is full of other souls who are hardy both with and without the 'fool' prefix. The water's heated but you won't want to linger for long on the lawn in that chill. But who cares? Each abridged length gives you a chance to look at something new in the architecture – the covered seating area, the bandstand, the chunky stone that finishes buildings round these parts. Gifted in 1936 by razor blade manufacturer George Herbert Lawrence, who made his money in a massive works down the valley in Sheffield, the pool has been a much-treasured part of life in this Peak District village and offers the one thing that all villages really cry out for – a cheap, welcoming public space, which brings people together.

BROCKWELL LIDO

Herne Hill, London

In 1995, Lucy Blakstad made Brockwell Lido the star of her extraordinary film for the BBC's *Modern Times* strand. *The Lido* was one of the first instances of the lido renaissance being documented. The touching film shows how important the 1937 pool was to the community, even showing a marriage taking place here. Libby Page's 2018 smash-hit novel, also called *The Lido,* is set here too and runs with the same premise, tugging at the reader's heartstrings with its tale of love, loss and the lido fighting against closure. In reality it did close from 1990 to 1994 but you'd be hard-pressed to believe it if you visited on a summer afternoon today. The wooden decking is packed with people, the café is a popular destination, and the pair of ex-council workers who took the place over, Casey McGlue and Paddy Castledine, are revered as local heroes.

SANDFORD PARKS LIDO

Cheltenham

The pride of the spa town of Cheltenham - a bucolic Georgian resort known for its literature festival and poised on the edge of the Cotswolds - Sandford Parks Lido gives Cheltenham a spring in its step every time spring comes round again (it's only open seasonally). Some lidos can feel rather hemmed in, with brick walls encasing the place and sunbathing space at a premium, but Sandford Parks is spacious, with long lawns, benches and picnicking places a plenty. The 50m (55 yard) main pool is joined by a kids' pool and art deco architecture around the edge from its 1935 birth. The spouting fountain is the symbol of the place, a kind of Spanish tribute to the power and beauty of water.

OASIS SPORTS CENTRE

Holborn, London

The Oasis is a fortunate moniker which says it all. In the hubbub of Holborn, one of London's busiest yet least understood neighbourhoods, lies a swimming pool which not only offers unexpected respite, but tells us stories about ourselves. The wonder in the eyes of first-timers is pronounced, more so if they are Londoners who never believed a public swimming pool could exist in such a dense part of the city. Outside, the Victorian streets are choked with traffic and tourists, inside all is mellow. An outdoor sauna overlooking the pool is perfect for colder days and there's plenty of concrete to lounge on during a heatwave. Only the taxi horns beeping outside can convince you of where you really are. The Oasis is testament to a glorious age of British building, the 1960s, where nothing was considered too good for the public – including a luxurious, centrally located pool, and the social housing blocks of the Dudley Court Estate for pensioners that curl around the site, and are a part of the original development plan. This is the one place you should tell visitors to visit if they want to experience a surprising and enlivening London slightly beyond the tourist trap of the West End.

TOOTING BEC LIDO

Wandsworth, London

One of the early London lidos, Tooting was so ahead of the curve that the word 'lido' hadn't even come into common usage in Britain when it opened in 1906; it was known simply as Tooting Bathing Lake. At 90m (98 yards) long, it's a stretch from one end to the other. Built by the unemployed, it was an early example of municipal socialism in action. In her fascinating book *Liquid Assets*, Janet Smith describes how the lido was plagued by rats and that the first lifeguard Alfred French dressed in a full suit, shirt, tie and cap, and managed to use his rowing boat – which was always moored in one corner of the pool – to save the lives of two drowning swimmers in 1907, winning a Royal Humane Society award for his troubles.

Chris Romer-Lee

Co-founder of Studio Octopi
and Thames Baths CIC,
Working on a floating lido for London

Why do you like lidos?

Despite spending most of my childhood
holidays on or in water, my parents never
took me to a lido. But then that was the
1970s and 1980s, when lidos were closing
fast due to shocking under-investment, and
swimmers flocking to the new verrucae-
ridden indoor leisure centres that we all
hate now! I've lived in London all my life.
I love London and couldn't imagine living
anywhere else. There are times when you
need a few hours away from things and
we each have bolt holes we head for in the
city. Mine almost always involve water. To
a lido where the city is excluded and just
for a moment it becomes all about the sky
and Côte d'Azur blues. Swimming at night
in London Fields or risking early April for
the first days of double figures without a
wetsuit. Where else in London can you feel
so intimate with the soul of the city?

Tell us about your plan
for Thames Baths

Thames Baths was founded in 2013 for an
Open Call competition seeking ideas for
the River Thames. I was in Zurich swimming
in the lake when I became aware of the
competition. It seemed so obvious back
then. Our mantra became 'Reintroducing
swimming in the Thames' after I met Caitlin
Davies who wrote *Downstream: A History of
Swimming in the River Thames*.

The initial plans were so well received
by the public that we developed two other
iterations and then launched a crowdfunding
campaign to fund development of the
idea. Thirty days later we had £142,000 to
employ consultants and begin to work out
exactly how we were going to achieve the
dream. We've had so much help and support
over the years. The campaign continues
despite the authorities resisting the idea.
The opportunity to get children, adults

and over sixties swimming in a heated, naturally filtered pool in the Thames is what drives me on. We cannot give up and won't give up. Every major European city has these pools and the citizens love them. It's about health and well-being; it's about keeping London on the map despite the political mayhem driving us all to the brink.

Is swimming in the Thames going to be safe and clean?

The pool will be naturally filtered using the finest European water-filtering technology. This will remove all the pathogens and silt. We'll then heat the water to make it as safe and accessible as it possibly can be. Allas Sea Pool in Helsinki is very similar to what we're trying to do. This has a heated, treated pool and the option to safely swim in harbour water.

You are planning to redevelop Grange Lido in Cumbria too. Tell us why that one is close to your heart.

Save Grange Lido community group got in touch when they saw Thames Baths and Peckham Lido. Their campaign to convince the local council to work with them on the restoration has been amazing. We have been a tiny cog in the all-powerful community. This lido is truly exceptional and it's a national embarrassment that it's been allowed to slip into such disrepair. I love the setting – the way it loops out from the town's promenade embracing the flat openness of Morecambe Bay so gracefully.

And you're proposing a Peckham Lido?

This has been another long-running project but again the initial drive has come from the community. At first we held a crowdfunding campaign and raised £66,000 through Spacehive. It's a very local campaign with the majority of the pledges coming from south-east London. The campaign allowed the client to pay consultants, including ourselves, to develop a viable design through community consultation. Our vision is to invert the 1930 lido. As opposed to building high, white-painted concrete walls around the pool, we're inviting nature in, retaining the mature greenery on the site (the site of the original Peckham Rye Lido until it was demolished in 1987) and mixing this with a beach and naturally filtered pool. There is even a plan to resurface the River Peck that was lost to a pipe under site after the war.

What are your favourite pools?

Lidos are magical but if I'm out of London I prefer a river or sea. I've obviously got a particularly sweet spot for floating lidos and have conquered Gothenburg and Helsinki so far. Zurich as the birthplace of Thames Baths has a big place in my heart and the river baths there are spectacular.

Do you admire classic art deco lido architecture?

I do but that was then and this is now. Less concrete, more timber and the inclusion of nature – that's the future. I'm looking forward to expanding London as a 'city of lidos' with a new generation of pools.

JUBILEE POOL

Penzance

The sheer abandon of Jubilee Pool is what stands out – you'd expect nothing less from something designed by a man who went by the title Captain F. Latham. The bravado is epitomized by the bold shape – like a huge Dorito or Toblerone slice – and by its size. This is the largest saltwater lido in Britain. Today that bravado continues: the people running the pool have drilled into the sea bed to provide the geothermal energy to heat its water. Clever stuff. Sat on the front in Penzance, Jubilee feels exposed and open to Mother Nature. This was all the more apparent in 2014 when freak waves destroyed this landmark and caused howls of anguish across Cornwall. But the Jubilee came back – repaired and more popular than ever. It's lived through a lot – opened in 1935 for George V's Silver Jubilee, it popularized Penzance as a resort in the art deco era.

Joe Minihane

Writer
Author of *Floating:*
A Return to Waterlog

How did you find that swimming could improve your mental health?

I came across swimming as a salve for my anxiety by mistake, really. As I mention in the book, my wife and I went swimming at Hampstead mixed pond one summer afternoon and it went from there. Beforehand, swimming for me was always about laps at the local indoor pool. Afterwards, it was a case of going up to Hampstead and to Tooting Bec Lido as often as humanly possible.

I realized that it made me feel calm and centred in a way that nothing else did. The cold played its part. That initial shock, followed by the need to accept that it wasn't going to get much warmer, and then the need to simply survive replaced the thoughts that were whirring through my mind at a million miles an hour. When I started swimming outside, I didn't really understand that I had anxiety and depression. The state

of grace I felt afterwards suggested to me that feeling low and being worried about everything all of the time were not normal. The fact that it was outside appealed massively – there was a sense of it being out of the ordinary, a chance to share space with nature and be 'part of the scene' as Deakin puts it in *Waterlog*.

How did you go from being scared to jump in the pool to swimming in wild seas and caves?

Gradually! I hated swimming at school, it was a trigger for what I now understand was some pretty bad anxiety. Diving into the unknown, not having control, none of that appealed to me. I didn't really swim at all in my early twenties. I could swim a serviceable head-out breaststroke, but nothing you'd call swimming in the true sense. Then I had the classic thing that all people in their late twenties get, worrying about turning thirty and not being in

good shape (obviously that sounds hilarious to me now!), so I started going to my local indoor pool in Balham. It was around this time that I was really feeling bad, my mental health was terrible, I was being really unkind to myself and shutting myself off from any kind of help. Slowly, I taught myself to do breaststroke properly, and then front crawl.

It was still very much exercise for me at that point, physical rather than mental. Then Hampstead happened, around the same time I read *Waterlog*, and that was it really. I liked the sense of survival when it came to wild swimming. That there was nothing else you could do. It could be a long meditative swim in a calm bay or getting knocked about by waves for a few minutes. It didn't really matter. There was a sense of conquering some pretty deep-seated fears, of showing my younger self that I was OK.

That's not to say I consider myself hardcore. I bow down to the ice swimmers and the long distance guys. I'm a small bloke who feels the cold easily – so I just go in for as long as it takes to feel good and then get out. Sometimes it works, sometimes my mind's a bit of a mess, but I always feel better in some way for going. I've never regretted a swim.

How did Roger Deakin influence you?

Massively. I read *Waterlog* after coming across Deakin in Robert Macfarlane's *The Wild Places*, where they go exploring a holloway in Dorset. I had a sense of him being this kind of wild uncle that I'd never known. *Waterlog* confirmed that. He was fearless, passionate and hilarious and just

what I needed at a time when I felt my professional life was a mess and my mental health was in bad shape.

I wanted a new project , so decided to set up a blog called Waterlog Reswum. I'm nothing like Deakin – I have a terrible habit of people-pleasing, don't like upsetting authority and don't have an encyclopedic knowledge of nature. But I felt by going to the places he'd swum, I could get closer to him (he'd died in 2006) and take some of his spirit on the road with me. I wound up hopping fences to swim in the Itchen near Winchester, stealing a swim in a private river in Yorkshire and generally jumping in wherever I fancied, with the very real sense that Roger was giving me the nudge needed. He made me a better person, less het up, less anxious.

Was it a massive mission to do the research for *Floating*?

I started thinking I could do it in nine months, like Deakin had. It took just shy of three years, although I did break my wrist in that time and started having therapy to help with my issues. That became a big part of the book, as it took a turn I wasn't expecting and forced me to confront some quite raw things about myself. It was hard to write about that stuff, but necessary.

I was swimming pretty much weekly in the last summer of doing it (2014 – my last swim was in April 2015). I had a spreadsheet of 77 places, some of which were no longer open (like Droitwich Brine Baths), or just too dangerous (Corryvreckan whirlpool). Then there was the fact I couldn't drive, so needed to take trains and cycle everywhere, or get my mates to ferry me around. Fortunately,

I had a cohort of amazing pals who love swimming – Molly drove me to Cornwall and then all over the county. My mate James drove me to North Wales for a single swim from London and didn't even get in, just kept an eye on the bags. My uncle drove me to Jura and took me across the island for hikes when I couldn't swim. It got thoroughly out of control in the best possible way.

What are your favourite places to swim in cities?

Hampstead mixed and men's ponds are both my absolute favourites, mostly because they blend wild swimming with easy city access. That said, Tooting Bec Lido has a special place in my heart: it was close to where I lived and I spent many afternoons lounging there, watching the hardcore go back and forth along its 91m (100 yard) pool.

Outside of the UK, I did an absurd 'five swims around the five boroughs' feature last year in New York and absolutely loved Astoria Pool. It's a massive pool right on the East River with amazing views and concrete bleachers where the US Olympic trials were once held. It was an egalitarian space, with an area for swimmers, one for senior aerobics and another for kids to go crazy. For me it summed up all that's perfect about lidos. I love Brockwell Lido and Cheltenham too. Also, the baths in Cirencester aren't big, but are hard to beat for looming architecture and a pleasingly old-school vibe.

How does swimming make you feel and why do you do it?

Centred. I was chatting with a therapist recently and told him how it got right to my heart. In the sense that when I got out and dried off, I could feel a deep sense of my heart space being cool and clear. Physically I felt cold, but mentally I felt my heart space was warm, calm and open for anything.

While I'm in the water, it's the feeling of being in the moment, of meditating on your breath, whether a wave is going to wipe me out, or simply watching a gull whirl overhead. I've lived in Brighton for three years now and swim all year round without a wetsuit. Dips are brief in winter, but my entire day is then much less frenetic and my anxiety is put into perspective.

I do it because it makes me feel more alive, more connected to the world and less unsure of my own being. Sometimes I still feel terrible, but for me a swim will almost always give me a greater sense of perspective. It's not for everyone, but I couldn't be without it.

Britain's Lost Lidos

From Blackpool to Worthing, Britain was once dotted with lidos. But in the second half of the 20th century, as the country was frantically building everything else from tower blocks to motorways, its lidos were closing. Perhaps it's apt to compare them to the railways, which were also considered outdated by some, and axed around the same time period. The official narrative is that usage declined, punters started holidaying abroad and indoor leisure centres took away custom. Take those reasons with a pinch of salt, though. Just as the railways were said to be archaic and their usage was apparently 'dwindling' there was a classic streetcar conspiracy at work – a simple desire to cut costs coupled with a loss of love for the (not especially) old that was the sad flipside of high modernism. As with much-missed rural branch lines and urban tram networks, many towns and villages would dearly love their lido back, and many regret the hairbrained decisions to shut them – which was almost always about saving money and sometimes about redeveloping sites.

Birmingham's Cannon Hill Park Baths was sacrificed for the Midlands Arts Centre in the 1960s. Other big cities like Derby and Southampton lost their lidos. Even tiny villages had lidos: like Wilby in Northamptonshire, which went in the late 1950s, and of course

Above: Larkswood open air swimming pool, Chingford, Essex in 1950.
Next page: Sea Bathing Pool at Southport, Lancashire, in 1943.

MAX DEPTH 9FT 0IN

No. 8

Above: Bathers at the Open Air Baths in Chiswick in July 1923.

many seaside resorts. Barry Island's Knap Lido closed in the 1990s and was filled in around 2004, yet locals have continued to campaign for it to be reopened. Brighton, Ramsgate, Lowestoft, Scarbrough, Great Yarmouth, Clacton, Southport and many more seaside towns killed off their outdoor pools. London still seems blessed with lidos – but the options were even better in the past. You could also find lidos at Croydon, Surbiton, Muswell Hill, Alexandra Park, Dollis Hill, Chiswick, Chingford, Edmonton and Tottenham – the latter fell on its sword for the famous Broadwater Farm housing estate. This depressing state of affairs is only elevated by the fact that it would seem unimaginable to close an outdoor pool in Britain today, just as no one is suggesting axing railway lines ever again. In fact we're bringing those branch lines back, and we're reopening the closed lidos. Today's architecture may be questionable at times but at least we value our pools. Pontypridd in Wales and Thames Lido in Reading have been given second chances. Grange in Cumbria, although saved for now from being destroyed, is in limbo – being restored but not, weirdly, as a swimming pool; an odd state of affairs indeed. For the lidos that disappeared in the 20th century, irreplaceable architecture and a priceless local amenity was lost in the name of false progress. Reliquaries remain – rectangles on maps, dips in the landscape, the sound of splashing on the breeze.

AUSTRALIA

BRONTE
ROCK POOL

Bronte

Evelyn Whillier's death in 2004 was a sad day
for the town of Bronte, where she was known
by almost everyone. Whillier was a pioneer
of women's swimming, taking part in the 1936
Berlin Olympics and winning a gold, silver and
bronze at the 1938 Empire Games. A plaque in
her name sits next to Bronte Rock Pool, where
Whillier lived out a quiet life after her moment
of glory, teaching the town's kids to swim
for the next 46 years. It was for this reason
that she remained so well-known, having
essentially taught almost everyone in Bronte
how to swim. And what a pleasure it must have
been to learn in the Rock Pool. Free to enter,
it is as spectacular as it is refreshing. Cut into
the cliffs, a sheer rock drop above the pool
was for years a popular place to dive from.
Today it's fenced off, lifeguards prowl, and
onlookers cover their eyes – but show-off lads
still jump fences and evade capture to chuck
themselves off the 10m (33ft) ledge, landing
with a splash below. What would Evelyn
Whillier make of it all?

ANDREW (BOY) CHARLTON POOL

Sydney

A fascinating history of Australia comes alive at the unforgettably monikered Andrew (Boy) Charlton Pool. You can cast an intrigued eye over most of the Royal Australian Navy's fleet moored at the nearby Kangaroo Island base, and wonder how this huge military installation has somehow held out against the property speculators' avaricious glances; a prime slice of Sydney real estate occupied by sailors, stocks and rusting machinery. A wall used to encase the pool here to prevent peeping Toms looking at the ships – evidently they don't care any more. Many iterations of this pool have existed. The first one in the 1820s was just bits of an old ship broken up and staked out. Robinson's Baths, a private enterprise, followed in 1838. Twenty years later the Fig Tree or Corporation Baths were opened by Sydney Corporation. The grand Domain Baths in an Edwardian style opened in 1908. The Dom was to be a scene of swimming history in 1924 when Andrew 'Boy' Charlton broke the 220 and 440 yard world records. The 1968 pool took ABC's name, as does the 2002 version. Today's pool is modern, free from fuss and perched above the waters of Sydney Harbour, clinging to the side of the park known as the Domain. A truly unique ten lengths.

WYLIE'S BATHS

Coogee

Where does the sea end and the baths begin?
An existential question perhaps, one to be
pondered with a stubbie as the sun dips down.
At Coogee's sea baths on the north side of the
bay, huge rocks vaguely enclose a rectangular-
ish pot of pure Pacific with more drama than
an episode of *Neighbours* ever managed.
But at the south end, past the female-only
McIver Baths, Wylie's is a private, family-run
joint that will warm the cockles. From the retro
lettering of its sign that makes you think of
Dirty Dancing summer camps, to the bowls of
sea anemones dredged from the pool, which
you're welcome to take home and feast on,
it's a peach. A terrace of wooden decking
rises on piles and curves with the cliffside,
and on this deck there's a café doing mean
bacon sandwiches. Drop down the steps and
a rocky tanning shelf falls away to a sea pool
which is fully enclosed with slick, seaweedy
surfaces and, during bluebottle season, dozens
of the little buggers riding in on the waves –
something else for the tireless and effortlessly
chilled lifeguards to pick out of the pool.

ICEBERGS

Bondi

Star of a million Instagram photos, Icebergs pokes tantalizingly out into the ocean, begging for a pic. When the frothy surf smashes over the pool walls, the striking visual effect is heightened. A few lengths here are understandably on many bucket lists, and it's an easy one to tick off because so many backpackers find themselves in Bondi on their first few days Down Under. Not a bad place to begin the journey of a lifetime, is it? Maybe it's because of the drunk backpackers diving in after dark, or the tourists going topless (*verboten*), or the endless other bothers the exasperated staff here have to deal with, or perhaps the fame of the place, that it all seems a bit stressful sometimes. The modern building behind the pool is nothing to write home about, but the restaurant on the top floor serves a great brunch, and the people running the show up there are golden.

Why I Swim

Lena Peacock
Sydney, Australia

Why do you swim?

I think that water is intrinsic to all Australians. Being in it, being near it, and looking at it. From an early age my love affair with water and swimming began. I grew up by the beach and have always gravitated towards living by water. My parents used to call me the fish because I often refused to get out of the pool when I was little. In Australia you are essentially thrown into the water at a young age and somehow the love affair, rather than fear, begins!

Where do you swim?

Beach and harbourside pools are my favourite. You get the experience of being outdoors, the sense of community and they're free! Beach pools allow the experience of the beach without being crushed by massive waves or surfers not paying attention.

Which pools do you love?

My favourite is Cremorne Point in Sydney Harbour. It's free, your view is the stunning Sydney Harbour, including the Harbour Bridge in all of her glory, and it's usually not too crowded. Being level with the harbour without the chance of having your toes nibbled on by a shark is my idea of heaven.

Do you like pool architecture in Australia?

I've always been drawn to the North Sydney Olympic Pool's architecture, which is juxtaposed to the industrial angles of the Sydney Harbour Bridge. The only way you would be able to get closer to swimming under the Harbour Bridge would be if you were dodging ferries literally beneath it. The contrast between old and new architecture, with the new alterations done by Hassell, is also striking. Icebergs at Bondi is also an iconic one, but being on the other side of Sydney means I don't get to visit it very often.

How does swimming make you feel?

To me nothing beats the feeling of a lazy breaststroke on a summer's day with the sunlight dancing on the ripples all around me. Absolute bliss! Swimming makes me feel weightless, carefree and like nothing else matters outside of this moment. I would spend all of my time in the water if I could! It's impossible to not smile while swimming. The sensation of water against skin while moving through it is unlike anything else.

Tell us your favourite swimming stories

Back at high school as part of our education with water we would all spend a day dressed in full clothing where we are pretty much thrown into the water to see if we could make it back out of the pool without drowning. A series of exercises, practice rescues – and other activities that a bunch of teenagers are generally not too excited about – followed. I vividly remember mine at the Curl Curl Beach outdoor pool, held on a day when the seas were a bit wild and big waves were crashing over the tiny concrete walls. Our surf lifesaving skills were put to the test when one of our teachers ended up fully clothed in the water. I don't think we ever let that teacher forget the experience. I've also witnessed many first-time swim lessons and quite a few... amorous encounters within the ripples!

MANUKA POOL

Canberra

Australia's capital was the first city in the world designed by a woman. Marion Mahony Griffin deserves a biopic or a statue at the very least as testament to this. Instead the city's lake is named after her husband and collaborator, Walter Burley Griffin. Marion worked in Frank Lloyd Wright's office and her novel 'bush city' with its sweeping parkways and low-rise architecture is eye-opening. With no beach – the equivalent of the church almost in Australian culture – they realized they needed a pool and built one next to the Manuka Oval cricket ground, that other Aussie sporting essential. The handsome Great Gatsby lines of Manuka Pool's facade includes playful shell motifs, which evoke the far-away sea. Inside a grumpy attendant will take your fistful of dollars to let you step back in time. Sun-bleached benches and retro warning signs abound ('Running and spitting not allowed'). Vintage photos hark back in time to the bathing belle contests of the 1950s.

NORTH SYDNEY
OLYMPIC POOL

Sydney

There are a few contenders around the
world for the swim with the best view, but
North Sydney must be on that list. From the
bleachers the first sight is jaw-dropping.
Sydney Harbour Bridge launches itself out
over the water and almost over the pool itself.
The pool has so much sloped seating (which
punters stretch out and sunbathe on) because
it was a venue for the 1938 Empire Games.
The architecture on the outside follows that
Sydney rule of slightly squat brick that doesn't
cry out for attention. But on the inside art
deco flourishes that evoke a kind of sea jazz
age predominate, with shells, cockatoos,
swordfishes and trippy colours throughout. It's
a nod perhaps to Luna Park next door, that
retro fairground, and it's best enjoyed with
music and a beer.

What Pools Mean
to Australia

No other country in the world has Australia's aquaphilia. Swimming is more than a hobby here, it's a way of life. The sea presents itself like a gift, tempting you to dive in. And the spectacular sea pools that dazzle at Caloundra and Newcastle offer a halfway house between swimming pool and ocean. Half the country lives near the beach, but that's only half the story. The sprawling suburbs of Sydney and Melbourne mean you can find yourself a very long car ride from the briny. Private pools dot backyards, each Aussie feels it is their right to have a detached house with a garden big enough for pool, barbie and somewhere to knock a cricket ball around – as much as it is to gobble a snag at a sausage sizzle on election day (elections come along more regularly than buses here).

But it's the public baths that unite people every day, not just pool party specials in the suburbs. The writer Christos Tsiolkas – whose novel *The Slap* rips suburban Australia apart in the most breathtaking way possible – swims at his local pool, Brunswick Baths in Melbourne and his writing is inspired by changing rooms and races and sundecks. His book *Barracuda*

Above: Steps leading to Wylie's Baths, Coogee.
Next page: Icebergs, Bondi.

focuses even more keenly on swimming. For him, 'The water forces you to think of your sexual self', and it's as much about the sweat, the muscle and the men as it is about the breaststroke. Tsiolkas also points out that pools were an Anglo Saxon symbol of Australia but that diving in at Brunswick showed a multi-racial side of a country where indigenous kids had not so long ago been banned from even entering Moree Baths. Samantha Riley blazed a trail for Aboriginal swimmers in the 1990s, and today's Australia wants its new Asian and Arabic citizens to swim as much as anyone else. Australia's pool culture was celebrated in one of the 2016 Venice Architecture Biennale's most convincing pavilions, with water that you could paddle in. Sydney's Aileen Sage Architects proffered a pool which allowed you to cool off from the sweat of the swamp that Venice festers upon, while listening to the voices of Tsiolkas, the great front crawler Ian Thorpe and that other titan of modern Australian writing, Anna Funder – describing their thoughts on this typically Aussie typology. We must see classic Aussie pools like Beatty Park in Perth and Beaurepaire in Melbourne as symbols of the country as much as the koala and kangaroo.

Above: Bronte Rock Pool.

Madeleine Waller

Photographer and author
of *East London Swimmers*

What do you like about lidos?

Swimming outdoors in winter – I have to say I am a lightweight and prefer a heated lido.

What inspired you to take your photos of swimmers?

I was struck by how different fellow swimmers can seem in the water to the way they appear once out of the pool and dressed. It's almost as though the pool is a space where we can express an alternative identity. I wanted to explore the way we perceive others depending on the way they present themselves in different environments.

The human body is quite a funny thing when you see it out in the cold by the pool in the winter, right?

It's just a human body, I love all the different shapes and sizes. The pictures are more revealing when people are dressed.

London Fields is my local lido and yours. Why do you like it?

London Fields Lido is a really special place, there is a real sense of community there, particularly in the winter, you will often find yourself chatting to a complete stranger in the outdoor shower. It's amazing to have a heated outdoor pool in the middle of London. I prefer it during the winter months when it's quieter and a more contemplative space. When it first opened, if you timed it right, you could have a whole lane to yourself. It's really crowded during the summer and difficult to swim laps, but a great place to take the children on a hot summer afternoon, it feels as though you're on holiday. It's also one of the few 50m (55 yard) Olympic pools in the area, most of the pools in the UK are so small you've barely done a few strokes and you've reached the end.

What did you learn from the project?

That people have lots of different reasons for swimming and that they quite often see it as a form of relaxation or therapy. Myself included.

Do you like swimming? Why?

I love swimming, it's exercise without too much strain. It's incredibly calming and helps keep you disciplined, particularly when you're self-employed. It's a great place to go on a cold winter's day when the endless grey sky is getting you down. I didn't really start swimming laps seriously until my adult life, most of which I have spent in Hackney. It was the perfect exercise during my three pregnancies. I didn't always love it, I have a memory of being thrown into the ocean by my father and told to catch a wave, I was terrified, I dog paddled and coughed and spluttered my way back to shore after being dragged under a huge wave, not sure I would ever come up again.

You're Australian. Which other lidos do you like in Australia?

There wasn't a lido where I grew up in Australia, just the ocean and a freshwater tea tree lake where we mostly messed around to keep cool in the summer. The word lido isn't really commonly used in Australia and wasn't something I was familiar with. Sydney has some of the most amazing lap pools in the world: there is a beautiful lido, Icebergs at Bondi Beach, which overlooks the sea; Andrew (Boy) Charlton Pool beside the Botanical Gardens; North Sydney Olympic Pool, which has amazing views of the Sydney Harbour Bridge; and the many ocean baths like Coogee's McIver's Women's Baths, the last remaining women's-only seawater pool in Australia. There is an amazing one-lane lap pool in a hotel in Melbourne, which has a glass bottom over the street so you can watch people walking beneath you as you swim laps.

Can you tell us why swimming pools are so important in Aussie culture?

You are not only expected to know how to swim in Australia, you are also supposed to be good at it too. Despite the size of Australia, 85 per cent of the population live within 50km (30 miles) of the coast, so I guess it makes sense to learn to swim at an early age, not to mention the heat. It can be pretty relentless during the summer and in some parts of Northern Queensland you can't swim in the sea at certain times of year because of stingers and box jellyfish. Swimming lessons were mandatory at school. A big part of the culture is the school swimming carnival where everyone has to compete in a race, so even if you weren't a strong swimmer you had to compete in an event, even if it was just the novelty race. We were told about rips that could drag you out to sea, always to swim between the lifeguard's flags, or sharks that could kill you, not to mention the 'slip, slop, slap' campaign against skin cancer, yet Aussies still love to swim.

USA

OHLSON RECREATION CENTER

Sea Ranch, California

The final scenes in TV series *Mad Men* where Don Draper is ensconced with a coastal cult in California, like so much of that sublime show, speaks so perfectly of an era and its grim mores. In 1970 – when Don finds his peace – others were doing likewise, like here at the Sea Ranch halfway up Highway 1 between San Francisco and Mendocino, where the Ohlson Recreation Center was well on the way to completion. The wooden buildings and bold shapes are modern yet somehow also aware of the environment. The Sea Ranch has a cultish, intellectual vibe; its architecture is also brainy. The pool by Moore Lyndon Turnbull Whitaker of Berkeley sets an almost brutalist aesthetic against pale blue, its ballsy central tower now sadly shorn of slide and steps, with oversized coloured lettering systems and sliding partitions to finish things off in style. The whole ensemble was built as a sheltering system from the Pacific winds.

153

NEPTUNE POOL

Hearst Castle, California

Julia Morgan was an enigmatic architect and so different from today's publicity-seeking machines. So little is known about her that it really is a truism to say that her work is her legacy. The first female architect in California, she designed a string of prestigious projects, and Hearst Castle's Neptune Pool is one of the peaches in the punnet. William Randolph Hearst was an eccentric (and obviously the inspiration for Orson Welles' *Citizen Kane*). In Hearst Castle, he got himself something that looked like a church from Seville or Segovia – complete with somewhere for a dip around the back, with Roman and Greek temples overlooking the water. Located on the coast in San Simeon, it was quite the confection. The pool was huge for its time – but, this being America, it was consistently enlarged after its initial completion in 1925. The intricate tilework by Albert Solon and Frank Schemmel sets the piece off. Like many of our examples it fell on hard times and needed major surgery in the 2010s. Now it's perfectly restored and even featured in the video for Lady Gaga's 'G.U.Y'.

JOHN C. ARGUE
SWIM STADIUM

Los Angeles, California

In a city like LA where pools are everywhere –
in gardens and on the roofs of top hotels like
the Freehand and the Dream – public pools
do not perhaps have the pull they do in other
cities. Do not ignore this one though. Built for
the 1932 Olympics and messed around with for
the ones in 1984: the Los Angeles (aka John C.
Argue) Swim Stadium is in LA's Expo Park, next
to the Coliseum, which also hosted both those
games and an American Football Team, the
Rams. Both venues will be back for the 2028
Olympics too. In the pool on the day I dived
in: 100 kids learning breaststroke; the world's
first female roadie Tana Douglas (an Aussie
who told me she'd just come from signing a
book deal to write a memoir about life on the
road with rock bands); 20 trainee lifeguards in
Baywatch bathing suits, and one pasty British
scribe enjoying the sun.

VENETIAN POOL

Coral Gables, Florida

This one-of-a-kind pool combines two distinct elements – the 'natural' setting of a former coral quarry (hence the name of the town – just outside Miami – that it's located in) and the theme park-esque tricks of 'sort of Spanish/ sort of Italian' pavilion architecture around the fringes of the pool that are oh-so Floridian and predictably kitsch. Imagine how luxurious this place would have been in the 1920s when it opened. That kitschy vibe from architects Denman Fink and Phineas Paist was a first back then too, although the typology has been repeated ad nausem since then, in places from Las Vegas to Macau, somewhat robbing the original of its power. The high diving boards, rock faces and waterfalls add drama to the whole piece – truly a fun-filled place.

WAIKIKI NATATORIUM

Hawaii

Oahu's incredible outdoor pool has a fascinating tale to tell. Known locally as 'The Tank', it was built to honour the memory of soldiers from Hawaii who served in the US Armed Forces in Europe during First World War. Opened in 1927, it was the pride of the Waikiki seafront. The first person to jump in was Duke Kahanamoku – the so-called father of modern surfing. Architect Lewis Hobart's design is unique in its stature – the beaux-arts archway emblazoned with 'The War Memorial' sits in between a run of bleachers that stretches down either side of the pool, which in turn are topped with huge urns. The massive pool is in a state of disrepair as of 2020, but the hope is that this sentence will one day be out of date. A massive campaign to save the heritage structure is under way, led by the National Trust of the USA who have dedicated it as a 'national treasure' and one of America's top 'at risk monuments'. Hopefully it won't be too long before swimmers are welcomed again.

MCCARREN PARK POOL

Brooklyn, New York

Another of those tales of 1980s woe –
McCarren Park Pool closed in 1984 and was
out of use until 2012. During that time this vast
space was a backdrop for films, music videos
and concerts. But as Williamsburg became
increasingly full of artisan coffee shops and
vegan bakeries, demand for the pool to be
reopened rose, and thankfully the city had not
bulldozed it. Located in McCarren Park on a
sprawling site next to the skate park it's one
of Brooklyn's most vibrant summer spots. But
you shouldn't have difficulty finding a space – it
was built for 6,800 swimmers back in 1936 as
part of the New Deal, and opened by mayor
Fiorello La Guardia, who gave his name to
New York's domestic airport. The unusual vast
brick arch by architect Aymar Embury II sets
off the whole ensemble.

Swimming in Art

David Hockney was born in Bradford, a masochistic city which dismantled a football team, a finance sector, its entire town centre and its mighty wool industry – oh, as well as its open-air pool at Lister Park. Not that the West Yorkshire weather ever made it quite as enticing as some of the world's other, more glamorous outdoor pools. But it was in California, not Calderdale, that Hockney's epiphany took place. His 1960s paintings of pools – *A Bigger Splash* and *Peter Getting Out of Nick's Pool* – electrified audiences, pushed the boundaries of acceptable (then) homoeroticism and sold for vast sums. They have resonated. A version of

Portrait of an Artist (Pool with Two Figures) hangs on the wall of equine cartoon anti-hero BoJack Horseman, albeit with a horse swimming rather than a man. The bather in these works is always trangressive: the derrières of Hockney's subjects descend directly from Manet's *Le Déjeuner sur l'herbe* where (naturally) the viewer was invited to check out naked women; now though, it is men. Critic John Berger never forgot to remind us that the gaze was always sexist, and always came from the male eye, whichever way it was pointed. One wonders what Berger would have made of *Baywatch*? The lustrous light and the ebullience of pool culture in Palm Springs and Los Angeles

Above: David Hockney with his painting Peter Getting Out of Nick's Pool.
at the Walker Art Gallery in Liverpool, November 1967.
Next page: Ian Falconer swims at his home in Los Angeles in 1978, in
a pool painted by David Hockney.

Premier Issue

MARCH 1991

$7.50

enchanted Hockney; he also painted the desert modernist houses they sat next to – the Lautner and Neutra minimalist masterworks. Hockney's posters for the 1972 Munich and 1984 LA Olympics both fetishize swimming. Hockney painted onto a pool too – decorating the floor of the Tropicana Pool at the Roosevelt Hotel in Hollywood with squiggles and swirls (don't bother trying to get into this one if you're not a hotel guest).

Other artists have made such marks: Ed Ruscha pimped his brother Paul's pool in Studio City with giant type reading 'Name:_ Address:_ Phone:_' like a form that needs filling in. Lawrence Weiner's message on the bottom of a pool reads 'Stretched As Tight As Possible (Satin) & (Petroleum Jelly)'. Even Picasso painted a pool in Marbella. Pools as art installations have been put forward by the likes of James Turrell, Leandro Erlich and Elmgreen & Dragset. Alfredo Barsuglia built a pool in the same Californian desert where Peter Watkins shot his anti-authority movie masterwork *Punishment Park* in 1970; a pool that punters were free to dive into – if they could track it down. It was easier to find the LA Museum of Contemporary Art's pool by Hélio Oiticica and Neville D'Almeida – another piece of 'pool as installation' art you could jump right into. What else makes a pool 'art'? If it's attached to interesting architecture like at Albert Frey's Frey House II in Palm Springs perhaps, or maybe to a mid-century motel like the nearby Westward Ho, which is now of course the Ace Hotel and groans every year during Coachella Festival under the weight of creatives in luminous sunnies gone wild.

Above: The Swimming Pool, *by Leandro Erlich, permanently exhibited at the 21st Century Museum of Contemporary Art, Kanazawa, Japan.*
Previous page, left: Ed Ruscha's pool art on the cover of Push maagzine.
Previous page, right: The sculpture of a 9.1m (30ft) swimming pool by artist duo Elmgreen & Dragset titled Van Gogh's Ear on display at Rockefeller Center in New York in 2016.

WORLD

KENNEDY TOWN SWIMMING POOL

Hong Kong

Swimming among the skyscrapers is an elevating (literally) experience at Hong Kong's foremost public pool on the west of Hong Kong Island at Kennedy Town. Catch a clattering tram down from Central and you'll spot the huge pool complex looming up with its zinc-clad sides. The Terry Farrell-designed pool (he made his millions working on numerous projects in HK and China) plays that classic Hong Kong trick of getting handy with levels. Swimmers ascend long escalators and at the top is the full-size, rooftop al fresco pool loomed over by dozens of high-rises but with panoramic views up the hills and over the harbour. An unmissable experience in the former colony (now Special Administrative Region) whose British heritage has left a legacy of swimming madness. People here love to take a dip – respite from the incessant office life, political turbulence and cramped flats that dominate existence here, perhaps.

PARNELL BATHS

Auckland, New Zealand

The largest open-air saltwater baths in New Zealand's biggest city, Parnell is a place that many in Auckland have fond memories of visiting on summer days when they were kids. The architecture is a little more workaday than the impressive Tepid Baths in the city centre but nevertheless the collection of pools and changing rooms, which has been modernized many times over the years, still has buckets of charm. The complex is located to the east of the city centre in Point Park, overlooking Judge's Bay. The 60m (66 yard) main pool is augmented by a chill pool and a slides complex. There's also a massive sunbathing area – other pools take note, extend your sun terraces. Open during the southern hemisphere summer.

KITSILANO POOL

Vancouver, Canada

They say everything's bigger in Canada – well, this is the world's second largest country. Space is hardly a problem, so it's no surprise we guess then that Vancouver chose to build this super-sized outdoor pool right by the sea in cosmopolitan Kitsilano, a suburb so boho that you're likely to witness *en masse* nudism down on the beach at almost any time of year (if it's warm). Just a stroll along from those dunes you can find this whopping 137m (150 yard) long public pool. In fact it's Canada's longest – three times as long as an Olympic pool. Kitsilano Pool dates from 1931, but was completely refurbished in 2018, uses saltwater and is only open in summer.

ENTRANCE to POOL

All BATHERS ENTERING POOL MUST
BE ENTIRELY FREE OF SAND or
PASSED by ATTENDANT
Eatables of All Description
STRICTLY PROHIBITED

SUNNYSIDE POOL

Toronto, Canada

Toronto's main outdoor baths were also Canada's biggest at the time when the doors were flung open back in 1925. The baths were an integral part of Sunnyside Amusement Park, which also featured rollercoasters, games and sideshows – but its presence down on the shores of Lake Ontario was testament to the fact that hardy souls had been taking dips in the lake here for decades. Indeed, the lavish, Alfred H. Chapman-designed Bathing Pavilion pre-dates the pool by some three years, and was for bathers to change in prior to jumping in the lake. But then it became attached to the pool. Sunnyside was essentially Toronto's riviera, but when the Gardiner Expressway was ploughed through and the amusement park closed in the 1950s, it slid into decline. The pool has soldiered on though and remains a summer treat for many Torontonians.

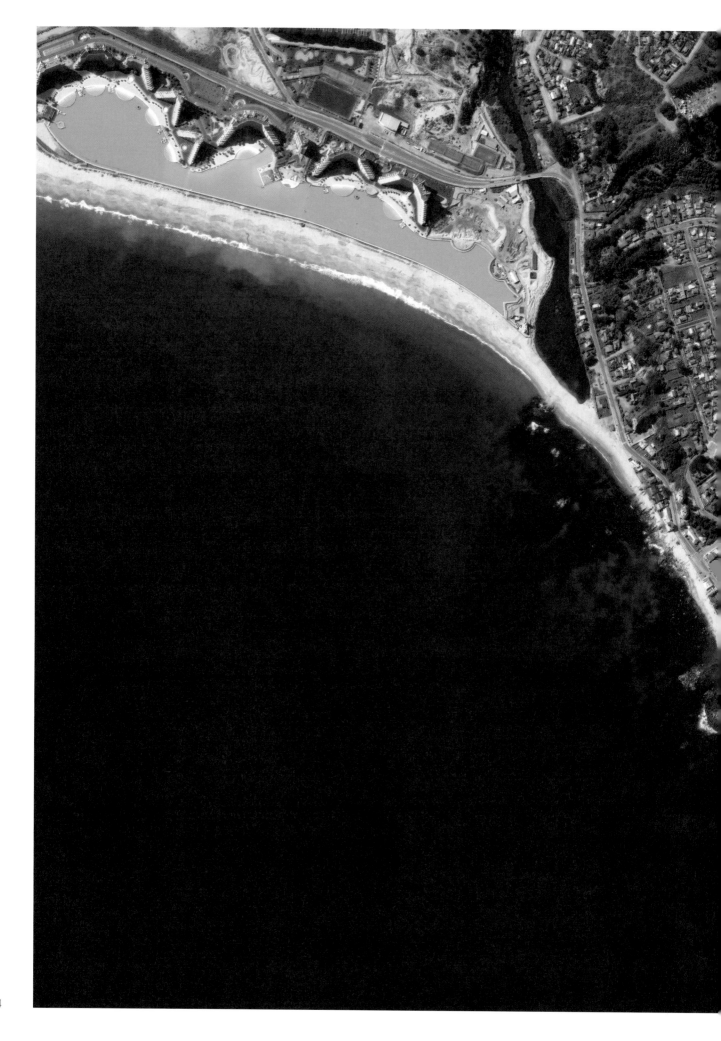

SAN ALFONSO DEL MAR

Chile

What an absolutely bizarre undertaking: in fact, here is the world's biggest swimming pool. Down in Algarrobo, Chile – Santiago's de facto seaside resort – lies this elephantine project. Why anyone would want to spend five years and £2 million digging a pool almost 1km (²/₃ mile) long and filling it with 250 million litres (55 million gallons) of seawater is a moot point, but anyway, they did it. In front of a sprawling apartment complex, between the buildings and the Pacific is this monstrous pool, which is so big it looks like a natural lagoon on Google Maps. They even let you kayak or sail from one end to the other. The pool at San Alfonso del Mar opened in 2006.

SEA POINT POOLS

Cape Town, South Africa

A collection of pools boasting an extravagant heritage diving board cluster, looked over by Table Mountain, and right next to the ocean – which is so shark-infested you'll want to swim here instead. What's not to love? Sea Point is a pleasant suburb of Cape Town, just west of the city's CBD (central business district), and this cute complex is a big draw. On clear days a swim here comes complete with a view that will sober you as much as the cold water – Robben Island out on the horizon, once the prison of Nelson Mandela and the other fighters against South Africa's apartheid regime, now a museum. If you've got a taste for it, Cape Town also boasts some appealing tidal pools around its foreshore: Camps Bay, St James, Saunders Rocks and Soetwater's twin pools are some of the most popular.

PHOENICIA HOTEL POOL

Beirut, Lebanon

Beirut's modern history is your classic three-act screenplay. The swinging Sixties were the apogee of its wild times. When Dubai was still just a few cottages, this was where the Middle East came to party. It didn't get any crazier than at the Phoenicia, whose modernist pool was the epicentre of the fun and games. Then came the devastating Civil War of the 1970s and 80s. The hotel district of the city presents a remarkable living history lesson today. A stroll around this area is like walking with ghosts – dozens of abandoned buildings; pock-marked, blown-up, falling down. The Phoenicia is still going though, refurbished and again trying to lure tourists to the city. You'll have to brave a metal detector to get in, but that pool is perfection on a hot Levantine afternoon, surrounded by Roman pillars à la Las Vegas and sunloungers where you can order drinks. Altered from its original modernist design it nevertheless still treats guests as if they were kings on a royal retreat.

Angela Elvira Bruce

Filmmaker
Director of *Lido*,
a film about Parliament Hill Lido

Tell us about the film you're making about Parliament Hill Lido?

Lido started as a study of a building and the social space it encloses, and how it changes through seasons. Being an open-air swimming pool and located in Hampstead Heath, its relationship with nature is very close, in a way, even exaggerated, creating a dramatic narrative arc – the winter is more serene, the summer more abuzz with energy and flashier than the surroundings. The art deco architecture, too, and the water were all readily cinematic. Yet equally important to me in the making of this film were the personal life stories of people involved with the building. I wanted to make a film that can commemorate or serve as an elegy for the late Glyn

Roberts, a lifeguard who worked at the lido for 25 years. The film was conceived as an ethnographic project for a graduate program at UCL under the mentorship of an acclaimed filmmaker Sophie Fiennes, but it has evolved into an obliquely intimate, meditative portrait.

Why do you love lidos?

I don't have a love for all lidos. This one in particular is special to me as it is steeped in personal history. My brother Alan was a seasonal lifeguard there for over 15 years and the community he built there are like family to him. I went to school in Highgate and the lido was a regular summer haunt, so in portrayal of the summer season in the film there are elements of autobiography.

I love the theatrical nature of lidos and observing all the different body shapes and sizes along with different styles of motion. The lido creates its own choreographies, patterns of movement that I wanted to capture in a film.

Do you always love swimming?

My brother and I trained at swimming hard as youngsters and competed in galas, so we've always loved the water. I have never been a cold water swimmer though. In fact, I did try to get a job as a lifeguard years before making the film and, being a strong swimmer, I thought the job was in the bag – after all, I was 'Alan's sister'. I didn't factor in the water temperature and on the day of the test I dived in and experienced cold shock syndrome, quite a traumatic experience! My body was so unaccustomed to the crushing temperature that I felt I was drowning. I decided the job was not for me, and the lido from that day forth took on a daunting persona in my mind. I guess you could say that I got over that experience, fell back in love with the place, and connected with the lido community through my camera.

Where else have you swum in the world?

I was born and raised in London, and my mother is from La Paz in Bolivia. My father hailed from Newcastle and was an engineer who went to Bolivia to help build a tea factory. I've swum in beautiful outdoor pools in Bolivia, particularly Santa Cruz. Once, I stayed in a mansion on the coast of Sicily, which had a private infinity pool. We could see Mount Etna on the horizon. It was so beautiful it felt hyper real.

What makes lidos in London special?

Every time I walk into the lido on Parliament Hill and see the water, my breath is taken away, and my pupils instantly shrink due to the light bouncing everywhere. The pool is bigger than Olympic size and kept in pristine condition. It is a sharp contrast to the polluted city life we are accustomed to. Lie on your back in the water and drink in the sky – you could be anywhere! The combination of connecting with nature, your own physicality, other people and the natural high you get from cold water swimming is empowering; it gets one ready for London.

WHERE TO FIND THEM

Naturbad Riehen
Weilstrasse 69
4125 Riehen
Switzerland

Islands Brygge Havnebadet
Islands Brygge 14
2300 Copenhagen
Denmark

Bains des Pâquis
Quai du Mont-Blanc 30
1201 Geneva
Switzerland

Piscine du Rhône
8 Quai Claude Bernard
69007 Lyon
France

Zollverein Mine Pool
Gelsenkirchener Str. 181
45309 Essen
Germany

**Piscina Municipal
de Montjuïc**
Avinguda Miramar, 31
08038 Barcelona
Spain

Blue Lagoon
Nordurljosavegur 9
240 Grindavík
Iceland

Freibad Mirke
In der Mirke 1
42109 Wuppertal
Germany

Zelena Zaba
17. novembra 297/15
914 51 Trenčianske Teplice
Slovakia

Allas Sea Pool
Katajanokanlaituri 2a
00160 Helsinki
Finland

Badeschiff
Eichenstraße 4
12435 Berlin
Germany

Piscina das Marés
Av. Liberdade
4450-716 Leça da Palmeira
Portugal

Piscine Molitor
4 Rue Nungesser et Coli
75016 Paris
France

Lake Bled Lido
Veslaška promenada 11
4260 Bled
Slovenia

Olympia Schwimmstadion
Olympischer Platz 3
14053 Berlin
Germany

Haludovo Hotel
51511
Malinska
Croatia

Alt-Erlaa rooftop pools
Anton-Baumgartner-Straße 44
1230 Vienna
Austria

Lido di Milano
Piazzale Lorenzo Lotto
15, 20148 Milan MI
Italy

Seebad Utoquai
Utoquai 50
8008 Zürich
Switzerland

London Fields Lido
London Fields West Side
London
E8 3EU

Bristol Lido
Oakfield Pl
Bristol
BS8 2BJ

Saltdean Lido
The Oval Park
Saltdean Park Road
Saltdean
Brighton
BN2 8SP

Tinside Lido
Hoe Rd
Plymouth
PL1 3DE

Parliament Hill Lido
Parliament Hill Fields
Gospel Oak
London
NW5 1LT

Hampstead Heath Ponds
Hampstead Heath
London
NW5 1QR

Stonehaven Heated Open Air Pool
Queen Elizabeth Park
The Links
Stonehaven
AB39 2RD

Hathersage Swimming Pool
Oddfellows Rd
Hathersage
Hope Valley
S32 1DU

Brockwell Lido
Brockwell Park
Dulwich Rd
London
SE24 0PA

Sandford Parks Lido
Keynsham Rd
Cheltenham
GL53 7PU

Oasis Sports Centre
32 Endell St
London
WC2H 9AG

Tooting Bec Lido
Tooting Bec Rd
London
SW16 1RU

Jubilee Pool
Battery Road
Penzance
TR18 4FF

Bronte Rock Pool
Bronte NSW 2024, Australia

Andrew (Boy) Charlton
1c Mrs Macquaries Rd
Sydney NSW 2000, Australia

Wylie's Baths
4B Neptune St
Coogee NSW 2034, Australia

Icebergs
1 Notts Ave
Bondi Beach
NSW 2026, Australia

Manuka Pool
New South Wales Cres
Griffith ACT 2603
Australia

North Sydney Olympic Pool
4 Alfred St S
Milsons Point NSW 2061
Australia

Ohlson Recreation Center
37405 Shoreline Hwy
Sea Ranch
CA 95497
USA

Neptune Pool
San Luis Obispo
San Simeon
CA 93452
USA

John C. Argue Swim Stadium
3980 Bill Robertson Ln
Los Angeles
CA 90037
USA

Venetian Pool
2701 De Soto Blvd
Coral Gables
FL 33134
USA

Waikiki Natatorium
2815 Kalakaua Ave
Honolulu
HI 96815
USA

McCarren Park Pool
776 Lorimer St
Brooklyn, NY 11222
USA

Kennedy Town Swimming Pool
Kennedy Town
Sai Cheung St, 2
Hong Kong

Parnell Baths
25 Judges Bay Road
Parnell
Auckland 1052
New Zealand

Kitsilano Pool
2305 Cornwall Ave
Vancouver
BC V6K 1B6
Canada

Sunnyside Pool
1755 Lake Shore Blvd W
Toronto
ON M6S 5A3
Canada

San Alfonso del Mar
G-98-F 886
Algarrobo
Valparaíso
Chile

Sea Point Pools
Lower, Beach Rd
Sea Point
Cape Town
8060, South Africa

Phoenicia Hotel Pool
Fakhreddine Street
Beirut
Lebanon

FURTHER READING

Art Deco Britain
Elain Harwood
(Batsford, 2019)

Barracuda
Christos Tsiolkas
(Hogarth, 2014)

East London Swimmers
Madeleine Waller
(Hoxton Mini Press, 2014)

Floating: A Return to Waterlog
Joe Minihane
(Duckworth, 2017)

Haunts of the Black Masseur: The Swimmer as Hero
Charles Sprawson
(Vintage, 2013)

Liquid Assets: The Lidos and Open Air Swimming Pools of Britain (Played in Britain)
Janet Smith
(Malavan Media, 2005)

The Lido
Libby Page
(Orion, 2018)

The Lido Guide
Janet Wilkinson and Emma Pusill
(Unbound, 2019)

Turning: Lessons from Swimming Berlin's Lakes
Jessica J Lee
(Virago, 2017)

Waterlog: A Swimmer's Journey Through Britain
Roger Deakin
(Vintage, 2000)

PICTURE CREDITS

© Alessandro Della Bella: pp. 8–9, 16–17, 64–65

© Agencja Fotograficzna Caro/ Alamy Stock Photo: p.30

© Alexander Rentsch: pp.56–57

© Agefotostock/ Alamy Stock Photo: pp.154–155

© Africa Drone Guy/ Alamy Stock Photo: pp.174–175

© Amanda Sigafoos/ Dunked in Public: pp.156–157

© Angela Elvira Bruce: p.192

© Bacchus PR: pp.190–191

© Bettmann/ Getty Images: pp.160–161

© Bill Oxford: pp.152–153

© Cinoby/ Getty Images: pp.2–3, 206–207

© Charlotte Bland: pp. 4, 6, 11, 68–69, 73, 84–85, 88–89, 96–97, 98, 99, 102–103, 111

© Chris Romer-Lee: p.106

© CCN-images: pp.58–59

© Col Ellis/ Gallery Twenty Seven: pp.138–139

© C & S Pictures/ Getty Images: pp.182–183

© Cultura RM/ Alamy Stock Photo: pp.188–189

© Craig Gibson: p.72

© Deborah Arthurs: p78

© Douglas Peebles Photography/ Alamy Stock Photo: pp.162–163

© DigitalGlobe/ Getty Images: pp.184–185

© Dpa picture alliance/ Alamy Stock photo: pp.28–29

© Elena Pejchinova/ Getty images: pp.54–55

© Fernando Guerra/ VIEW: p.46, p.47.

© Gosia/ Alamy Stock Photo: pp.36–37

© Giovanni Russo (designer) and Paul Ruscha (photographer)/ PUSH Magazine: p.170

© Hemis/ Alamy Stock Photo: pp.32–33, 50–51, 53

© Howard Davies/ Alamy Stock Photo: pp.140–141

© Illustrated London News Ltd/ Mary Evans Picture Library: p.118

© Iwan Baan Studio: pp.18–19

© Julia Gavin/ Alamy Stock Photo: pp.104–105

© Joe Minihane: p.110

© John Shepherd/ Getty Images: pp.108–109

© JaCZhou/ Getty Images: pp.22–23

© Jason Kwan/ Alamy Stock Photo: pp.180–181

© Jon Arnold Images Ltd/ Alamy Stock Photo: pp.186–187

© Lena Peacock: p.136

© Liz Eve/ Fotohaus: pp.74–75

© Leon Foggit/ Getty Images: p.205

© Madeleine Waller: p.148

© Mary Evans Picture Library/ Grenville Collins Postcard Collection: p.116–117

© Mary Evans Picture Library/ Gerald Wilson: p.115

© Museum für Gestaltung Zürich/ ZHdK: p.24

© M. Sobreira/ Alamy Stock Photo: p.25

© MARKA/ Alamy Stock Photo: pp.62–63

© Mike Twigg, fotocapricorn/ Alamy Stock Photo: pp.80–81

© Melanie Watkins: pp.125, 128–129, 130, 131, 132–133, 134–135, 143, 144–145, 147

© Model10/ Alamy Stock Photo: pp.126–127

© Mauritius Images GmbH/ Alamy Stock Photo: pp.150–151

© Marco Cattaneo/ Alamy Stock Photo: pp.158–159

© Mirrorpix/ Getty Images: p.167

© Marcel Lam/ Farrells: pp.176–177

© Michael Childers/ Getty Images: pp.168–169

© Nano Calvo/ Alamy Stock Photo: p.173

© Natalie Dawkins, with kind permission of Orion Books: p66

© Pete Hill: p.92

© Pixabay: pp.40–41

© Philip Bier/ VIEW: pp.20–21

© Prisma by Dukas Presseagentur GmbH/ Alamy Stock Photo: pp.34–35

© Pro Mirke e.V: pp.38–39

© Photononstop/ Alamy Stock Photo: p.52

© Peter Erik Forsberg/ Alamy Stock Photo: pp.42–43

© Rebecca Armstrong: p.86

© Reppans/ Alamy Stock Photo: pp.76–77

© Riekephotos/ Shutterstock: pp.178–179

© Ryan Pierse/ Getty Images: pp.120–121, 122–123

© Steve Vidler/ Alamy Stock Photo: pp.82–83

© Simon Price/ Alamy Stock Photo: pp.90–91

© Simon Van Hal: pp.60–61

© TravelibUK/ Alamy Stock Photo: pp.94–95

© Timothy A. Clary/ Getty Images: p.171

© Ullstein Bild/ Getty Images: pp.44–45

© UPI/ Alamy Stock Photo: pp.164–165

© View Pictures/ Getty Images: pp.46–47

© Viennaslide/ Alamy Stock Photo: pp.26–27

© WENN Rights Ltd/ Alamy Stock Photo: pp.70–71

© Zoonar Gmbh/ Alamy Stock Photo: p.31

© Yves Andre/ Getty Images: p.124

© Sandford Parks Lido pp.100–101

THANK YOU

All the people who kindly agreed to be interviewed in the book: Rebecca Armstrong, Lena Peacock, Libby Page, Chris Romer Lee, Angela Elvira Bruce, Pete Hill, Renay Richardson, Madeleine Waller, Debs Arthurs. Ines Fressynet for letting me write about lidos for Euronews, Ben Spriggs for commissioning my piece in *The Guardian* about lidos back in 2014 and Julia Buckley for willing me to write about them for *The Independent* in 2017. Csilla Letay for German insight, Joe Minihane for kind support, Nicky Trup for encouraging me in, all the people who joined me poolside in 2019 like Kate Wills, Clare McQue, Kirsty McQue, Andre Mcleod, Jason Sayer, Faye Caldwell, Jodie Cramphorn. The staff and swimmers of London Fields Lido who are always so cheery, and everyone else at lidos around the world who've welcomed me. My parents and brother for always being encouraging. Alessandro Della Bella, Charlotte Bland and Melanie Watkins for their photos. Lilly Phelan for organizing the wonderful pictures in this book and everyone else at Batsford – especially Frida, Gemma, Tina, Polly and most of all my brilliant editor Lucy Smith.

INDEX